Museum Master Planning

Museum Master Planning
Basic Principles and Best Practices

Guy Hermann and Sara Patton Zarrelli

ROWMAN & LITTLEFIELD
Lanham • Boulder • New York • London

Rowman & Littlefield
Bloomsbury Publishing Inc, 1385 Broadway, New York, NY 10018, USA
Bloomsbury Publishing Plc, 50 Bedford Square, London, WC1B 3DP, UK
Bloomsbury Publishing Ireland, 29 Earlsfort Terrace, Dublin 2, D02 AY28, Ireland
www.rowman.com

Copyright © 2025 by The Rowman & Littlefield Publishing Group, Inc.

All rights reserved. No part of this publication may be: i) reproduced or transmitted in any form, electronic or mechanical, including photocopying, recording or by means of any information storage or retrieval system without prior permission in writing from the publishers; or ii) used or reproduced in any way for the training, development or operation of artificial intelligence (AI) technologies, including generative AI technologies. The rights holders expressly reserve this publication from the text and data mining exception as per Article 4(3) of the Digital Single Market Directive (EU) 2019/790.

British Library Cataloguing in Publication Information available

Library of Congress Cataloging-in-Publication Data Available

ISBN 978-1-5381-9262-7 (cloth: alk. paper)
ISBN 978-1-5381-9263-4 (pbk.: alk. paper)
ISBN 978-1-5381-9264-1 (electronic)

For product safety related questions contact productsafety@bloomsbury.com.

♾️™ The paper used in this publication meets the minimum requirements of American National Standard for Information Sciences—Permanence of Paper for Printed Library Materials, ANSI/NISO Z39.48-1992.

Dedication

For my wife, Jo-Anne, who helped give form to the ideas that underpin this book, and for E. Verner Johnson, who helped me to grow and develop as a museum master planner.
(GH)

For Chelsea, who believed in the book before it was "the book."
(SPZ)

Contents

List of Figures, Resources, and Templates		ix
Acknowledgments		xi
Preface		xiii
Chapter 1:	It's All about People	1
Chapter 2:	The Three Types of Museums	9
Chapter 3:	The Practical Foundations of Master Planning	19
Chapter 4:	Benchmarking: Learning from Others' Success	25
Chapter 5:	Identifying the Museum's Constituent Groups	37
Chapter 6:	Developing the Constituent Logic Model	45
Chapter 7:	Activity and Experience Planning	57
Chapter 8:	Staffing and Operational Needs	73
Chapter 9:	Facility Planning	83
Chapter 10:	The Master Plan and Next Steps	99
Chapter 11:	What *Really* Happens Next?	111
Index		115
About the Authors		121

List of Figures, Resources, and Templates

Figure 0.1	Space Allocation Chart for the Academy Museum of Motion Pictures	xiv
Resource 1.1	John Cotton Dana, excerpt from *The New Museum* (1917)	5
Figure 2.1	Guitar Pick Diagram	12
Figure 2.2	Operating Implications for Destination, Community, and Curatorial Museums	13
Figure 2.3	Guitar Pick Diagram for the Academy Museum of Motion Pictures	14
Figure 2.4	Guitar Pick Diagram for the Center for Puppetry Arts	15
Figure 2.5	Guitar Pick Diagram for the Art Complex Museum	16
Resource 3.1	Sample Resources, Constraints, Challenges, and Opportunities Summary	23
Template 4.1	Museum Financials Tracking Table	31
Template 4.2	Museum Attendance and Entry Fee Tracking Table	31
Template 4.3	Museum Staffing and Facility Tracking Table	32
Resource 4.1	Benchmark Interview Questions	34
Resource 5.1	Brainstorming Session Homework Template	41
Resource 5.2	Interview Candidate Selection Checklist	42
Resource 5.3	Tips for Scheduling and Conducting Interviews	42
Resource 5.4	Sample Interview Discussion Guide	43
Template 6.1	Logic Model Template	46
Resource 6.1	Logic Model Described in the Chapter	51
Resource 6.2	Sample Completed Logic Model	54
Resource 7.1	Excerpt of an Activity and Experience Plan for an Historic House Museum	66
Resource 7.2	Excerpt of an Activity and Experience Plan for a Mid-Sized Museum	68
Template 7.1	Activity and Experience Plan Template	72
Template 8.1	Staffing Assessment Table	77
Table 9.1	Preliminary Capital Budgets for Three Different-Sized Museums	87
Table 9.2	Sample Site-Selection Scoring Table	88
Template 9.1	Facility Assessment Table	89
Table 9.3	Sample Assessment of a Museum Classroom	90
Resource 9.1	Preliminary Museum Space List	92
Resource 9.2	Site Evaluation Worksheet	94
Table 9.4	Sample Site-Evaluation Score Sheet	96

Acknowledgments

The approach to museum master planning described in this book is the result of over twenty-five years of hands-on experience helping museum staff and boards to develop their own master plans. Because museums succeed in so many different ways, every project helps us to hone the approach to master planning outlined in this book still further. We appreciate all the clients over the years who have allowed us to learn with them. In particular, the following projects significantly sharpened our thinking: the Academy Museum of Motion Pictures, the Apollo Theater, the Art Complex Museum, Connecticut Landmarks, the Emily Dickinson Museum, the Eric Carle Museum of Picture Book Art, the Flint Hills Discovery Center, the Martha's Vineyard Museum, Museum L-A (now Maine MILL), the National Museum of African American History and Culture, and the New York Academy of Medicine. In addition to these projects, we have been fortunate to work with many other consulting professionals, including architects, exhibit designers, and a wide variety of other types of planners whose insights and skills have helped bring our master plans to life.

We also received feedback during the proposal process for this book from three anonymous reviewers. Each reviewer provided thoughtful feedback on the ideas that have shaped the manuscript. The book is surely better for it. The authors would also like to thank our editor, Charles Harmon, and assistant, Lauren Moynihan, for their assistance in bringing the book from an idea to the work you now hold in your hands.

Guy Hermann:
This book owes a significant early debt to my mentor, E. Verner Johnson, museum architect and planner. Verner, unlike many architects at the time, understood the value of investing in master planning before beginning architectural design, especially for museums. His pragmatic approach to master planning valued every part of the museum, from collections storage to the loading docks. Verner's work provided a solid foundation for the approach to master planning outlined in this book. I am particularly grateful to Verner for accepting my contention in the interview process for my first position as a museum planner that my experience as director of information technology at a major museum gave me a broader and deeper understanding of the ways museums worked than any of the traditional museum disciplines. I hope that some of his DNA is embedded in this book and continues to help shape museum architectural practice.

How to acknowledge my wife's contributions? Perhaps the best way is with a story. When Jo-Anne and I worked together for a few years, we always began our projects with in-depth interviews with a wide variety of stakeholders—ranging from board and staff members, the mayor, and, perhaps, the newly minted curator. In one of these meetings for a museum in Vermont, a board member was describing the impact a museum program had on some young people he knew. I dutifully made a note on my legal pad, nodding my head as I did so. At the end of the day, Jo-Anne asked me if I had seen it. "Seen what?" I asked. "That he was crying!" "He was . . . ?" I asked. I had indeed missed the tears. I was so focused on the details that I failed to catch the emotional context. I am still working on learning that lesson.

A special thanks goes to my three children, who grew up with a museum planner as their dad. They provided valuable insight into how younger visitors interacted with museums and were exceptionally patient when Dad had to take a few extra minutes to see how the loading dock was arranged. (This is still a running family joke.)

This book would not be here without Sara, my co-author. There is no way I can capture all the ways that she has helped bring the book to life. First by believing it could happen, and later, by making it happen: organizing and pitching an outline, writing first drafts of all the chapters, organizing the work plan, and cheerfully keeping my feet to the fire when deadlines loomed. Working together on the book, while simultaneously working together on a wide variety of master planning projects (from the Art Complex Museum to a museum for the US Coast Guard), gave us ample opportunity to learn from each other and enrich the content of this book. And all of it with good cheer and a clear sense that we could get it done. I couldn't think of a better partner.

Sara Patton Zarrelli:
When I arrived at the Rowman & Littlefield table at the National Council on Public History Annual Meeting in 2023, my only intention was to buy a copy of the recently released *Change Is Required: Preparing for the Post-Pandemic Museum*. While no copies were available, Charles Harmon noticed the "award-winner" label on my name tag and struck up a conversation about the award-winning work for Connecticut Landmarks that led directly to this book. While Guy and I had discussed the idea of a book several times, it is unlikely that we would have written it without this fortuitous conversation. Thank you, Charles.

Writing, even with a co-author, may be a solitary affair, but it takes a community to bring a writing project to a successful conclusion. Many people have supported the process beyond those named here. Rebekkah Rubin offered early thoughts on the publishing process and proposal content, all while working on her own writing. Together, we have shared the ups and downs of writing, editing, and publishing, and I'm grateful for her perspective and (at times) commiseration. Chelsea Clifford believed in this book before it was even "the book," and her belief that that it would both be finished and be worth publishing has been a source of inspiration. Likewise, Serena Zabin, my longtime mentor at Carleton College, retained a breezy confidence that "of course you'll finish the book." My family, especially my parents, Mary and Charles Patton, have long supported my plan to make a career in the museum field, and I am thankful for their enthusiasm and encouragement. My husband, Joe Zarrelli, deserves special mention for supporting the writing process with many cups of tea, reminders of the critical importance of the Oxford comma, and consistent noting of my habit of omitting articles. Beyond the writing process, my life is richer for his presence, and I'm grateful to have him as my partner as we travel through life.

Last, this project could not have been completed without my co-author, Guy Hermann. I have had the great fortune to work with Guy for several years through a wide range of unusual and interesting projects that have allowed me to learn and grow in both expected and unexpected ways. Beyond these, he has unfailingly supported my professional growth and encouraged me to pursue opportunities and projects that interested me. This book project has been one of many adventures we have had together, and one that I hope adequately captures the methodologies Guy has developed over the years and shared with me.

Preface

In our work as part of a consulting firm that specializes in master planning for museums, we can't say we've seen it all, but with more than fifty museum master planning projects under our belts, and a combined thirty years of museum master planning experience, we have seen a lot of different ways that museums can be successful. Our goal in writing this book is to pass on the many lessons we have learned about museums, how they operate, and the unique ways in which each one can succeed.

The thinking behind the master planning process we have outlined in this book began with the development of a master plan for an organization operating four distinct museums located in one city and under one organizational name. The museums include an art museum, a natural history museum, a science center, and a pop art museum. At first glance, it seems all museums have much in common—they combine exhibits, collections, programs, a gift shop, and often, a café. It may seem to some that the only difference is size. But this project quickly put that idea to rest. A cursory review of these four museums revealed that "small," "medium," and "large" weren't going to cover the vast differences between them. The art museum needed to bring together its original nineteenth century building with its relatively recent modernist addition. The natural history museum had not had a substantial renovation since it was built and needed significant updates to the visitor experience and its collections storage and work areas. The science center was packed to the gills with families on weekends and needed more space. And the pop art museum was already outgrowing its relatively new location.

This project was a crash course in how different museums can be, and it provided an ideal introduction to the complexities of master planning for museum building projects. How would it be possible to put the very different needs of these four museums into a coherent master plan? For the planning team's leader at that time, it was simple: Ask the museum staff what they needed. Document those needs. And then organize the needs into a structured space plan. But what about the museums' actual users? The visitors, researchers, members, contributors, and others? Where did they fit? How were their needs met?

The role of a museum's users in master planning became clearer a few years later with work developing a major African American museum. Perhaps the most important question posed to the commission charged with developing a preliminary plan for the museum was, "Who is this museum for? The African American community, or all Americans?" This question provoked a lively discussion and ended up with a consensus that the museum should be for all Americans. After only a few projects, it was becoming apparent that perhaps the most important question to ask was, "Who is this museum for?"

The value of this question crystalized with planning work for a film museum. The preliminary concept was to create a tourist destination for visitors to Los Angeles. The group developing the museum had already begun to buy land in Hollywood and planned for a major tourist destination with tens of thousands of square feet of interactive exhibits and immersive experiences. With that as a goal, the preliminary budget was similar to that of a high-end action movie. But as the work progressed, it became clear that many of the stakeholders would also like the museum to include a state-of-the-art one-thousand-seat movie theater, big enough for movie premieres, with an event space nearby that could accommodate a reception for all the premiere's guests. With that addition, the construction budget ballooned to that of three or four action movies. It became a priority to get the desired building in line with the budget.

Discussions with the museum's planning team brought into focus that the question was not, "What should we build?," but, "Who are we building this for?" More than a million people in Los Angeles work directly or indirectly for the film industry, and it was evident that the museum needed to be located closer to the people who would be its primary supporters. As important, the museum's exhibits had to live up to the quality of the work that it takes to win a major award. Efforts to balance the program and the budget revealed that reducing the area (and funding) devoted to long-term exhibits would free up sufficient funds to support the one-thousand-seat theater that would best serve the movie-industry regulars who would become its patrons. Figure 1 shows how the allocation of space changes between a tourist-focused museum and a museum designed primarily to serve the film community. Once it was clear that the capital cost would be essentially the same for either option, the community-focused scheme became the preferred option. The Hollywood properties were sold off, and the organization elected to redevelop a site adjacent to a major art museum, where it has become a center for film-related exhibits, programming, and events.

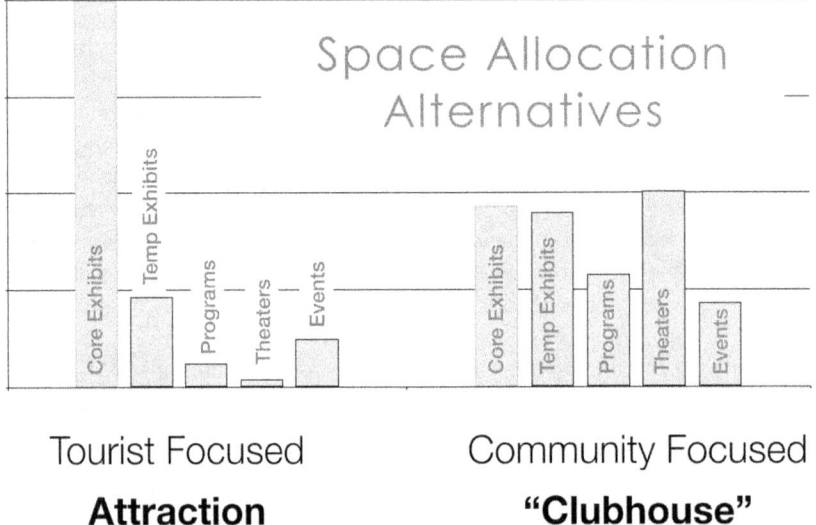

Figure 0.1 This table compares the space allocation for a tourist focused vs a community focused musuem. Note which areas change most as the musuem's focus shifts. Museum Insights

Master planning work for what began as a tourist attraction and would evolve to become a regionally noted science center cemented the user-focused approach to museum planning. The project had begun as a municipal project designed to attract tourists to a small city in the Midwest. Funding was in place through a state regranting program, and the team's charge was to develop a master plan that could be implemented immediately. In the initial meetings, the team was surprised to learn that a prior consultant had recommended "Tornado World" as a sure draw for tourists. It hardly needs to be said that this was not a popular concept locally. Worse was that the new team of consultants brought in to implement a new scheme was presumed to be of the same ilk, and the consulting team was greeted with deep suspicion and a bit of outright contempt. But as more background research was completed, it became clear that the region's truly distinctive characteristic was the fact that it has the densest coverage of intact tallgrass prairie in North America. The prairie is managed by the National Park Service and the Nature Conservancy in partnership with local ranchers and is also home to a very significant biological research center managed by the state university. Despite the special nature of the regional prairie, community members knew little about the unique ecosystem in their own backyards.

The team's new proposed concept built on research by the National Park Service and scientists at the research center to shape an indoor nature discovery center in the middle of the city designed to engage residents and visitors with the region's unique prairie environment. The locals embraced this community-focused concept, but the additional challenge was that the state funding source required that more than 50 percent of the museum's visitors come from more than one hundred miles away. To meet this requirement, the exhibit design team created an immersive environment, complete with simulated thunderstorms and prairie fires every half hour in the building's atrium and exhibit spaces. The result is a must-see destination, a significant community learning resource, and a much greater appreciation of and respect for the prairie by both local residents and visitors.

This project cemented our understanding that *museums differ primarily in whom they serve*, not in what they have or what they do. Further, museums succeed when they can understand and articulate how each of three broad categories of constituents are most important to their success. These three categories are:

- *Destination* constituents, who are visitors, typically from out of town, who are primarily interested in engaging experiences and compelling stories. They are engaged by long-term exhibits, and, increasingly, immersive experiences. Destination constituents often only visit once and can be a source of earned income.
- *Community* members, who are largely local residents, who often have an ongoing relationship with the museum, attending programs, visiting regularly to see what is new, and supporting the museum with membership and annual fund donations.
- *Curatorial* constituents, who typically have a research or professional interest in the museum's collections or archives. Curatorial constituents may include collectors, scientists, and others interested in specific collections or artifacts. Curatorial Museums are most often supported by endowments or as part of research organizations like universities.

These three groups, and their many minor variations, have proven to provide a solid foundation for understanding and then meeting the needs of a wide variety of museum constituents in an equally wide variety of museum contexts. Perhaps the most useful outcome of this approach is its ability to bring museum planning team members (board members and staff) to consensus about their museum's primary constituents, and how the museum's collections, exhibits, and programs can best help meet these constituents' unique interests, needs, motivations, and desires.[1]

Throughout the book, we will explore this and other critical aspects of museum master planning, including:

1. *Understanding Constituents:* Identifying and understanding the interests, needs, motivations, and desires of various constituencies is crucial in planning and designing activities and experiences that foster meaningful engagement. Meeting the needs of key constituents is critical to a successful museum.
2. *Business Planning:* Determining and estimating sources of revenue, staffing needs, and operating costs that are aligned with the museum's priority constituents ensures that a museum can balance its books after opening.
3. *Master Planning:* Developing a master plan that aligns with the museum's mission and vision lays the foundation for long-term success. A successful master plan includes a detailed constituent

analysis, Activity and Experience Plans, operating projections, site selection criteria, space plans, estimated capital costs, and other details or plans critical to the project's success.
4. *Balancing Vision and Pragmatism:* Striking the right balance between visionary ideas and practical considerations is essential for the success of any museum project. Setting realistic goals, ensuring stakeholder alignment, and maintaining financial sustainability are important at every stage of the planning process.
5. *Phases of Museum Development:* Understanding the different phases of museum development, from the initial idea and master planning to architectural design, construction, and operation, allows planning and design teams to move forward with confidence, knowing that they can adapt plans as the need arises.
6. *Sustainability and Adaptability:* Planning for long-term economic and environmental sustainability and for changing circumstances prepares a museum to be resilient. Considerations include anticipating future needs, incorporating flexible design elements, and ensuring ongoing relevance to the community and stakeholders.

Our ultimate goal for this book is to provide museum professionals with the tools and insights needed to successfully navigate the complex process of museum master planning. By detailing planning methodologies and drawing on real-world examples, we aim to empower readers to create museums that are not only culturally and educationally significant, but also financially viable and deeply connected to their constituents.

Whether you are embarking on a new museum project or seeking to reinvent an existing institution, this book will serve as a comprehensive guide to clarifying and communicating your vision and making a lasting impact in the world of museums. Through careful planning and thoughtful execution, museums can become enduring cultural landmarks that educate, inspire, and connect people across generations.

NOTE

1. We use the term *constituents* here very deliberately, as it embraces the wide variety of local residents, tourists, families, program participants, collectors, researchers, and the many other groups who might engage with a museum.

1

It's All about People

As glimpsed in the preface, planning a new museum, or updating an established museum, is a complex process. The museum master planning process described here is designed to simplify, clarify, and focus planning for the museum by engaging multiple stakeholders and identifying not how the museum will operate ("What should we collect?") or what it will look like ("Who will be our architect?"), but whom the museum will serve ("Who are our most important constituents?"). Of course, the easy answer to the last question is, "We do it for the visitors!" But which visitors? Art lovers? Families with children? Local residents? Friends visiting town? Members? Volunteers? Enthusiasts of your story? Collection aficionados of multiple sorts? Sometimes answering these questions is easy. Consider children's museums and science centers. Both focus primarily on the children of local residents, and their business models are built on memberships and repeat visitation. Children's and science museums are easy to replicate, and we find both types of museums operating in similar ways across the country. They make it seem almost easy to run a museum. But for most museums, audience and constituent questions are more complex, and the possibilities can seem endless.

Take, for example, a museum like the Eric Carle Museum of Picture Book Art in Amherst, Massachusetts. Designed as a place to celebrate the art of picture books, the museum followed the typical conventions of an art museum—white box galleries and diffused natural light. And, while they did get many art lovers, it turned out that one of the most common visitor groups consists of several three- or four-year-old *Very Hungry Caterpillar* fans and their parents and, frequently, their grandparents, seeking to engage their children in the art and books that they loved as children. The museum also was surprised to find that dozens of other picture book artists were anxious to donate work to the museum, quickly maxing out the collection storage space available. Then the museum's traveling exhibit program took off, shipping artwork around the United States and as far away as Japan. How do you balance and prioritize such unique and differing programs and needs when there is no cookie-cutter model to follow?

Here, we make the case that successful master planning for museums encompasses collections, exhibits, and programs, but it begins with people. A strong master plan is built on a deep understanding of the interests, needs, motivations, and desires of the broad spectrum of people who care about the museum—visitors, donors, board members, staff, volunteers, neighbors, and many other groups unique to specific museums. Our experience affirms the theories advanced by museum pioneer John Cotton Dana, and management practices from business leadership expert Peter Drucker, and we use them to ground our planning practices. A short introduction to their work will provide a foundation for the activities in the chapters ahead.

John Cotton Dana first articulated many of the ideas that are a foundation for modern public libraries and modern museums. Dana's father was a prominent minister, but John, uninterested in the ministry, chose to pursue law school. An illness derailed his studies, and he traveled westward working a variety of jobs. In 1889, chiefly on personal connections, he was appointed the librarian for the Denver Public Library. Dana took the library by storm and quickly made significant policy changes. Innovations included open stacks with good lighting and reachable shelves, branch libraries, and greater access to all by offering extended open hours and library cards for any resident. Dana also introduced the first dedicated children's room, featuring children's artwork in addition to books, marking the first time that children were encouraged to visit libraries.[1]

Dana was a creature of the progressive era and believed that the changes he was making in the library supported many of goals of the progressive movement, especially expanded access to education and enhanced citizen engagement with their communities. At the core of Dana's reforms was the idea that citizens needed access to information to contribute to a democratic society. As such, libraries had no role in limiting or censoring the kinds of books and information citizens could access at a library. Dana's beliefs were put to the test when populists suggested switching the nation's currency from a gold to a silver standard. The switch would have benefited Colorado, which had extensive and productive silver mines. Despite strong silver sentiment locally, Dana continued to make "gold-bug" literature available for those who asked for it at the library. Backlash to his support for open access to information prompted him to return to the East Coast in 1896, where he led the Springfield, Massachusetts, library, before accepting a position in Newark, New Jersey, in 1902. He chose to move to Newark because he hoped that the job would allow him to continue his library reform while also pursing museum work, which he believed was intertwined with the purpose of a public library.[2] He viewed his role at the Newark Library as a chance to test new museum models within the library and, eventually, to develop a new and useful stand-alone museum for the city of Newark, which opened in 1909.[3]

Dana began by conducting a survey of museums operating in the United States. He was disappointed by the results. Reporting on his findings in 1917, he concluded, "A very brief study of these museums and the use made of them in adding to the pleasure, to the broadening and enlightening, and to the definite education of their respective communities, convinced us that they are among the least effective products of community enterprise that American development has brought forth."[4] When he said "these museums," Dana meant the whole universe of museums, from art galleries to "conventional scientific and historical and industrial collections."[5] Based on his assessment, Dana decided the only thing to do was to build a new model for museums from the ground up. The model Dana developed was radical.

He began by considering what other civic and commercial enterprises effectively met the needs of their patrons or constituents and which of these methods might be adapted for the museum. Dana sampled a wide range of institutions, concluding in *The Gloom of the Museum*, "A great city department store of the first class is perhaps more like a good museum of art than are any of the museums we have yet established." While he did eventually conclude that "a department store is not a good museum,"[6] he called out museums for their dogmatic exhibit presentation, which he summed up as "look, trust the expert, and admire."[7] If a museum wanted to improve its engagement, then it should consider what department stores do well: they are open during the hours patrons want to visit; things are well lit and attractively displayed; it is organized according to the needs and interests of its patrons; and it provides information and assistance to all its visitors. For Dana, no operational model was out of bounds provided that it made museums a force for public education and engagement in their own communities.

Dana believed that an effective museum reflected the interests and characteristics of its community. He called for working cooperatively with both established collectors in the community and supporting citizens, especially youth, interested in developing collections to exhibit. As such, collections in Dana's ideal museum leaned heavily toward demonstrating "objects which are products of the community's activities in the field, factory and workshop."[8] Exhibits were intended to engage young people with the work of the older members of their families, stimulate creativity and craftmanship, and even engage businessmen, potentially attracting investment into the community. Dana was also a fierce advocate for taking the museum outside of its own walls. He called for practices that are common to museums today: sharing museum objects with schools to support and enliven teachers' lessons; installing exhibits in convenient and accessible areas, including in schools and business districts; and loaning objects that would otherwise be in storage to other institutions for display and study.[9] Dana put these ideas into practice in Newark and reflected on their success in *The New Museum* (1917). He began that book by defining eleven principles based on his work in Newark (see Resource 1.1 for the complete list,) and he then provided a series of templates, recommendations, and contacts for others looking to establish museums in the model he proposed. For many museum professionals, these eleven principles still resonate and are present in the mission and goal statements of a wide variety of museums. Understanding those whom the museum serves and how the museum can best engage its community members must be at the heart of any successful planning process.

This concept of understanding the communities an organization serves was also articulated by Peter Drucker, who wrote extensively on leadership and management in both for-profit and nonprofit organizations. Drucker was born in Vienna and worked as a reporter while completing his doctorate in public and international law. He began his career as an economist and in banking in Vienna, but he fled Hitler's advance into Austria in 1933. He first went to Britain, and then, in 1937, he moved to the United States.[10] Once in America, he turned his focus toward business, studying General Motors for two years. The resulting book, *Concept of the Corporation* (1946), argued that great companies are among humankind's best innovations. The book launched him to international fame and a career as a professor and consultant, with an increasing interest in improving the management of nonprofit organizations. In 1990, he published *Managing the Non-Profit Organization: Practices and Principles*.[11] Drucker was the first to convincingly argue that nonprofits needed to acknowledge that they were businesses. Their measure of success was not their bottom line, but how well they fulfilled their missions and drove positive change. He noted that nonprofits played a critical role in American life by providing services that the government did not, engaging community members in volunteerism, and accounting for 2 to 3 percent of the nation's gross national product.[12] He argued that achieving positive results as a nonprofit was more challenging than simply delivering a profitable bottom line because a nonprofit's product is a "*changed human being*."[13] To achieve their missions', nonprofits must exercise tremendous focus and discipline.[14]

The impact of *Managing the Non-Profit Organization* was significant, and the work was developed into a workbook for nonprofits to help them assess their management techniques. Likewise, a posthumous work called *The Five Most Important Questions You Will Ever Ask About Your Organization* distilled the ideas presented in *Managing the Non-Profit*. These questions are:

1. What is our mission?
2. Who is our customer?
3. What does the customer value?
4. What are our results?
5. What is our plan?[15]

Drucker called for a continuous assessment cycle that begins by considering the nonprofit's mission. He posited that first, the organization must drill down to the most simple and succinct statement of its goals.[16] Drucker went on to argue that every successful enterprise—whether a business or a nonprofit—is successful because they understand the needs of their customers and provide products or services that meet those customer needs. Drucker saw nonprofits as having two customers: "The *primary customer* is the person whose life is changed through the organization's work. *Supporting customers* are volunteers, members, partners, funders, referral sources, employees, and others," who also must be satisfied.[17] Drucker urged nonprofit leaders to focus on their primary customers and keep their description of that customer simple and specific. This allows the organization the most focus, and in turn, the most opportunities to change lives.

Once the customer is identified, the organization must then understand what that customer values. Drucker defined *values* as "what satisfies their [customers'] needs, wants, and aspirations," which can only be identified by asking the customer directly.[18] Using the example of an organization serving unhoused people, Drucker pointed out that when the organization spoke to the people they served, what they wanted more than meals and overnight shelter was "a place of safety from which to rebuild our lives." The organization shifted their services to better address this value and saw more success in assisting unhoused individuals.[19] Having identified the organization's mission, primary customer, and primary customer's values, the organization can now assess its results.

First, the organization must determine what should be assessed, and then assemble both qualitative (stories) and quantitative (data) research that allows for assessment. Then, the organization must act on the results, asking the question, "Do we produce results that are sufficiently outstanding to justify putting our resources in this area?"[20] Drucker urges organizations to look beyond both tradition (the organization has always done this) and need (there is a need for this service or program) because effective management means allocating resources to the areas of most impact, even if it means discontinuing programs that are traditional or needed. This is hard. Drucker writes: "To abandon anything is always bitterly resisted."[21] Yet, often nonprofits can only effectively achieve their missions by letting go of what isn't doing the most good and focusing on the results their customers truly value.

Drucker's final assessment step is to develop a plan that draws the first four questions together, defining the organization's mission and setting a few clear, long-range goals that will accomplish the mission. These goals become guardrails that help keep an organization on track by defining the kinds of activities that are most important to pursue.[22] The five questions provide a road map to keep any nonprofit organization innovating and moving forward to best meet the needs of its customers and in turn its own mission.

Taken together, the ideas of Dana and Drucker suggest that museums will be successful at engaging and inspiring their visitors when they fully understand the needs of the people whom they want to serve. Today's museums face challenges distinct from any Dana or Drucker probably could have imagined:

- bringing underrepresented groups to the museum;
- reckoning with previous or all-too-recent episodes of racism at the museum (whether its collections, its exhibits, internal practices, or visitors services/security);
- being responsive to repatriation activities;
- changing interpretation to reflect a broader range of ideas, cultures, and experiences;
- determining how to appropriately address collections that were collected unethically or stolen from their countries or cultures of origin;
- collecting and displaying human remains;
- creating and sustaining an equitable workplace;
- and many more topics that, taken together, form a formidable list of challenges and opportunities for change.

How are we to tackle these kinds of problems with the advice of two dead, privileged white men? Because their methods—if not their examples or all of their own beliefs—still hold power. Drucker is adamant that the only way to truly serve a constituency is to ask them what they need and provide it.

If museums are serious about serving new constituencies, then we must get to know them and meet their needs, *as they describe them to us*. We can't continue to guess what we think they might want. Nor can we continue to simply make sweeping proclamations about valuing diversity. Dana's advice still holds, too—museums should be places people come together for both education and entertainment. By many measures, as a field we've yet to fully embrace the level of change Dana proposed for museums a hundred years ago.

If change is going to occur, museums must understand the needs of their customers—as well or better than Dana's imagined department store or the unhoused groups Drucker describes. Our goal in this book is to help you to understand the particular groups your museum can most effectively serve, how to discover their needs, and how to develop this understanding into a long-range museum master plan that will help you make the kinds of changes you wish to see in your museums and that we all wish to see in the museum field. In the chapters ahead, we will walk through the steps necessary to understand those whom your museum serves and complete a people-centered planning process.

RESOURCE 1.1: JOHN COTTON DANA, EXCERPT FROM *THE NEW MUSEUM* (1917)

John Cotton Dana articulated eleven principles the effective of museum in *The New Museum*. They are reproduced here because they are still clear and recognizable to museum practitioners over one hundred years later.[23]

1. Entertain, and be ready to try to interest and instruct, such as may have the wish and the time to visit casually the institution's headquarters.
2. Entertain and more definitely and generally instruct, in classes and conducted groups, by labels, leaflets, handbooks, talks and illustrated lectures, such adults as may be induced to come to see special exhibits, also at the institute headquarters.
3. Entertain, interest and still more definitely instruct children who may be sent to the institute's headquarters from schools on stated occasions, and for certain specific observations; the objects observed, and the talks and the reading expounding the objects, being closely related to school work and to the age and stage of mental development of each group that comes.
4. Prepare for schools single objects and groups of objects with such labels, leaflets, lantern slides and instructors as the proper use of each may demand, and lend those to schools as the school authorities may designate; all being fitted, of course, to make easier the work of teaching and to make broader and more effective the work of the pupils.
5. Place in schools, as opportunity and fit occasions and the felt need of teachers, supervisors and the management may indicate, single objects and large and small collections of objects, fully labeled and accompanied by pictures, leaflets and pamphlets; all being such as may entertain and instruct both teachers and pupils, and particularly such as may be found to give constant and almost daily assistance in adding interest and values to studies and in broadening the experiences of pupils and in awakening new interest in them. These [are] to be changed as use and circumstance suggest.
6. Place in convenient and easily accessible rooms, like store rooms on business streets, and in special rooms with separate entrances in school buildings, single objects and small, well-rounded collections in art, science, industry, ethnology and other fields, such as experience shows will attract a large number of visitors. Manage these branch institutes, when possible, as veritable independent teaching centers, with leaflets and cards descriptive of the

museum's work and its acquisitions for distribution, and with skilled attendants who can describe and instruct as opportunity offers.
7. Discover collectors and specialists and experts in the community and secure their cooperation in adding to the museum's collections; in helping identify, describe and prepare labels and leaflets; in arousing the interest of young people in the museum's work and in finding such boys and girls as may wish to make collections of objects of any kind for themselves or for the museum. This development of the collecting habit among the young, with its accompanying education of power of observation, its training in handwork, its tendency to arouse interest theretofore unsuspected even by those who possess them, its continuous suggestions toward good taste and refinement which lie in the process of installing even the most modest of collections, and its leadings toward sound civic interest through doing for one's community a helpful thing—this work of securing the cooperation of boys and girls, making them useful while they are gaining their own pleasure and carrying on their own education, is one of the coming museum's most promising fields.
8. Lend to individuals, groups and societies, for any proper use and for any reasonable length of theme, any of the museum's objects, whenever it is clear that things thus lent will be of more service to the community than when they are resting, relatively unseen and unused, in the museum's headquarters.
9. Prepare and display, at the headquarters, at branches and in schools, carefully selected objects which are products of the community's activities in the field, factory and workshop. These will be local industry exhibits. They may be so small as to show in a very easily transported case a few of the major steps in the manufacture of a simple object. They may include merely a group of completed objects, interesting for their beauty or complexity, or for the high technical skill of the craftsman who made them. Or they may be so extensive as to fill every available inch of space the museum controls and to illustrate many aspects of one field of industry; and so general as to give a bird's-eye view of all the industries of the whole community. These may be planned to attract and interest the business man, or to draw to them the women, or to arouse in young people a healthful curiosity in the activities of their community and the results of the daily labor of men and women—their fathers, mothers, brothers and sisters, in the field, the store and the factory.
10. Keep the museum and its activities continually before the community in the daily press, and publish and distribute as many leaflets, posters, broadsides and cards descriptive of the museum's acquisitions as conditions seem to warrant. At the proper time publish leaflets and booklets, based on the museum's material, proper to be used as reading lessons in the schools.
11. Connect the work the museum may do, its objects and all activities of its staff, with all the resources of the public library. In doing this, many books and journals will be displayed near objects on view, references to books and journals will be made on labels and in leaflets of all kinds, and the library will be asked to show placards and notes and to distribute things the museum may publish descriptive or the purposes and activities.

NOTES

1. Kevin Mattson, "The Librarian as Secular Minister to Democracy: The Life and Ideas of John Cotton Dana," *Libraries and Culture*, Vol. 35, No. 4, Fall 2000, 518–19.
2. Ibid., 519.

3. The museum still operates and is now known as the Newark Museum of Art. The Newark Museum of Art, "A Museum and Its City," The Newark Museum of Art, https://newarkmuseumart.org/about/about-us/ (accessed November 3, 2023).
4. John Cotton Dana, *The New Museum* (Woodstock, Vermont: Elm Tree Press, 1917/Google Books, 2007), 12–13. https://books.google.com/books?id=DY1MAAAAMAAJ&printsec=frontcover&source=gbs_ge_summary_r&cad=0#v=onepage&q&f=false.
5. Ibid., 13.
6. John Cotton Dana, *The Gloom of the Museum* (Woodstock, Vermont: Elm Tree Press, 1917/Google Books, 2007), 23–24
7. Ibid., 24.
8. Dana, *The New Museum*, 17–18.
9. Ibid., 18.
10. Peter Drucker and others, *The Five Most Important Questions You Will Ever Ask About Your Organization* (San Francisco: Jossey-Bass/Wiley, 2008), xviii.
11. Peter F. Drucker, *Managing the Nonprofit Organization: Principles and Practices* (New York: HarperCollins, 1990), xvi.
12. Ibid., xiii. At the time Drucker published, he stated that "With every second American adult serving as a volunteer in the non-profit sector and spending at least three hours a week in non-profit work, the non-profits are America's largest 'employer.'" Levels of volunteerism have substantially decreased since 1990; according to recent census data only 23 percent (less than one in four) Americans report formally volunteering. While this could be considered a slow decline, the COVID pandemic is thought to have exacerbated it. These statistics will feel familiar to any organization that relies on volunteers and has faced increasing struggles to recruit and retain volunteers. This aside, we still expect nonprofits to fill some critical gap-filling work, leaving Drucker's argument to stand. Erin Schneider and Tim J. Marshall, "Volunteering in America: New Census Bureau/Americorps Research," United States Census Bureau, https://www.census.gov/library/stories/2023/01/volunteering-and-civic-life-in-america.html#:~:text=Related%20Statistics&text=The%202021%20Volunteering%20in%20America,was%20estimated%20at%20%24122.9B.&text=The%20U.S.%20Census%20Bureau%20and%20AmeriCorps%20announced%20the%20release%20of,(CEV)%20Supplement%20Microdata%20File (accessed October 20, 2023).
13. Drucker, *Managing the Nonprofit Organization*, xiv; emphasis original.
14. Drucker and others, *Five Questions*, 2.
15. Ibid., xii.
16. Ibid., 13.
17. Ibid., 25, emphasis original.
18. Ibid., 39.
19. Ibid., 40–41; Drucker uses the term *homeless*; we have updated the language to *unhoused* in the summary sections.
20. Ibid., 54.
21. Ibid.
22. Ibid., 69–70.
23. Dana, *The New Museum*, 15–18.

It's All about People

2

The Three Types of Museums

Museums come in many different forms. The archetypal museum sits at the top of a grand staircase with massive columns and a pediment akin to a Greek temple. A few museums do just that, but in real life, museums take many forms, ranging from natural and cultural history museums to classical and community art museums, from science centers and children's museums to academic and research museums, from nature centers to zoos and public gardens, and many, many others. Some museums operate with a full professional staff and a generous budget, while others run on a shoestring and depend on the good work of volunteers. Despite this abundance of museums, it is fair to say that no two museums are exactly alike and that there is no single model for a successful museum. The challenge in a master planning process is to uncover the operating model that will be most successful for each individual museum.

As we saw in Chapter 1, we believe that effective planning requires a people-centered process. The heart of a people-centered planning process is understanding those whom the museum (or museum-like organization) serves. In this chapter, we put forward a simple model for defining different types of museums and the groups of constituents they serve. Then, we explore how this typology helps to guide the activities of the museum, including collections, exhibitions, programs, funding, staffing, and operations. We will conclude with some case studies showing how real museums fit into these types.

Regardless of type, all museums share a single important commonality: they are seeking to reach specific groups of people, even if this is not explicitly stated in a museum's mission. Understanding and prioritizing the multiple groups that each museum serves provides the foundation for developing a master plan that identifies the components needed to make the museum successful. When you understand those whom you serve, you can more effectively define the activities that will meet their needs. It is tempting to bypass this step by simply declaring that the museum is for "everyone." But a critical point is that no museum can serve "everyone" effectively. Recognizing that is a good thing! Being everything to everyone is not a viable strategy for any organization. Seeking to serve everyone means that you cannot fully meet any group's needs and will likely deliver a disappointing experience to, well, *everyone*. Consider a restaurant with a menu that spans a dozen pages and multiple cuisines. Some things you can order from the menu are standouts. Others are not. How much better could the restaurant be if it focused on what it did best and left the lackluster eggplant parmesan to someone else?

Actively choosing *not* to serve everyone may seem counter to every museum's sincere desire to inclusively share exhibits, programs, and activities with the world. However, when we look more closely, we can see that museums are already tailoring their programing to specific groups. A museum might say, "We welcome everyone," and really mean it. But welcoming everyone is not the same as providing an exceptional experience that fulfills the interests, needs, and desires of every person coming to the museum. Children's museums, for example, strive to welcome a wide range of visitors with differing abilities, languages, and other characteristics as part of their mission to serve young children. However, this warm welcome probably wouldn't be extended to a single adult visitor without children in tow. Their presence would make the museum's primary visitors—children and their adult caregivers—uncomfortable. Welcoming, then, has its limits.

With this in mind, we need to make sure we are serving our most important constituents, or, as Peter Drucker would call them, our customers. As we discussed in chapter 1, Drucker argues that businesses and nonprofits thrive when they meet the needs of their customers. We translate this idea to say: "Museums thrive when they meet the needs of their constituents." But who are these constituents? What is it that they need? Why does understanding their needs help a particular museum to thrive? The work of answering these questions is at the heart of the master planning process. One tool that allows us to quickly understand our primary constituents and the operating models that serve them best is to divide museums into categories. Through our work, we have identified three broad categories of museums which we call "Destination," "Community," and "Curatorial."

DESTINATION MUSEUMS

A Destination Museum's constituents are primarily casual visitors, often from out of town. Destination Museums offer unique and engaging experiences with a big "wow" factor. Typically, they are places that a visitor wants to experience at least once in their life—bucket-list experiences that visitors may be willing to travel long distances to see. Often, they are places where families or groups of enthusiasts go to have experiences together, and a strong social element is incorporated into the exhibits and nearby amenities including special themed restaurants and shopping venues. A key aspect of a visit to a Destination Museum is making memories. In some ways, they can be thought of like tourist attractions that actively seek to attract visitors through the innovative design of their building, highly visible location, and richly engaging activities. Destination Museums can be important drivers of economic development or tourism in an area. Examples of Destination Museums include places like Halls of Fame, the Smithsonian Museums, and the iconic art museums. They can also include brand experiences like the World of Coke and military museums like the Marine Corps Museum. Visitors may be driven by a desire to have a specific experience ("I want to try the tasting room at the World of Coke that everyone is talking about.") or because they are passionate about the subject and seek to immerse themselves in it ("I've been fascinated by space travel all my life, and Space Center Houston lets me see where it all happens."). Since visitors come irregularly or even generationally ("I brought my kids and now I am bringing my grandkids."), the core exhibits, which are the primary offering at Destination Museums, do not change often. There may be a few temporary exhibits, but they are not a primary focus. The core exhibits are usually striking, immersive, and unusual, and they require a refresh every five to ten years to maintain the "wow" factor and stay up-to-date with changes in technology or our understanding of the world. Often, exhibits have a strong experiential storytelling bent to them. Destination Museums frequently have high ticket prices and rely heavily on earned revenue to support operations. Occasional capital funding is needed to support periodic exhibit refreshes that are needed to keep visitors coming and provide the kind of experience that destination visitors are seeking.

COMMUNITY MUSEUMS

Distinctly different from Destination Museums, a Community Museum's constituents are primarily residents from the local area (regional community constituents) or part of a group that has a specific interest in a museum's focus (affinity community constituents). Most museums are primarily regional Community Museums. In most cases, their mission (often unstated) is to connect people to the museum and to each other. A hallmark of Community Museums is activity—exhibits and programs are always changing and are designed to bring together the communities they serve for learning, for fun, or to engage in shared interests and activities. Unlike Destination Museums, Community Museums receive significant repeat visitation as visitors return to see the latest exhibit or attend a new program. Community Museums must be easily accessible to their constituents—easy to find, with ample parking or easily reachable by public transit, and universally accessible. Note that physical prominence is less important to a Community Museum—as long as the building is accessible and the parking is ample, community members will happily make their way to its location. A primary indicator of success for a Community Museum is ongoing involvement. Where Destination Museums typically use attendance as a primary metric, a more useful metric for a Community Museum might be member visits or the percentage of members in the local community.

It can often be useful to further distinguish the regional community and affinity Community Museums. Regional constituents are residents within a specific area around the museum who find the museum an important touchstone for the programs, events, and temporary exhibits that community members find engaging. Examples of regional community groups served by this type of museum include families with children, residents of the area, or retired individuals. Regional Community Museums may take many different forms; children's museums, science centers, history centers, and historical societies/historic house museums may all be regional Community Museums. Affinity community constituents, on the other hand, have a particular interest in a museum's specialty, particularly their specialized collections. Examples of affinity community constituents include lovers of Emily Dickinson's poetry (the Emily Dickinson Museum), collectors of American watches (the American Clock and Watch Museum), and current and former military service members (the National Museum of the US Army). For both affinity and community constituent museums, changing activities and repeat visits help the museums form long-term relationships with their visitors. These relationships in turn can provide a substantial portion of the museum's operating funds, through membership, annual funding, and legacy giving, in addition to support from an endowment or local or regional foundations or government entities.

CURATORIAL MUSEUMS

Curatorial Museums are primarily interested in collecting, curating, caring for, and providing access to a wide variety of collections objects, ranging from the world-class collection of fleas (yes, fleas) at the Carnegie Museum of Natural History to the paintings at the Clyfford Still Museum in Denver. Many academic museums are Curatorial Museums, with their specialized collections developed as part of academic research activities that are kept in storage with only a tiny fraction occasionally displayed in hallway wall cabinets. Users of Curatorial Museums are most often researchers or connoisseurs/collectors themselves. Exhibits and programs, the mainstay of Community and Destination museums, are a low priority for Curatorial Museums, and they are often open to the public on a very limited basis. As preservation and research are top priorities, these museums place security and anonymity over accessibility, meaning that they are often tucked away and not advertised. Likewise, Curatorial Museums change slowly, if at all, because their focus is on preserving collections and providing access to scholars and researchers who can make new discoveries using the collections. Curatorial Museums typically receive most of their funding from endowments or are part of a larger institution, like a university, that funds the museum's operations out of its larger budget. The Harvard Peabody Museums are a good example of a Curatorial Museum. While it is somewhat known for its remarkable glass flowers from its botanical collection, they are much less known for the dozens of other collections and the curators and scholars who care for them and conduct research.

Of course, no museum is just one type. We think of the three categories coming together as a kind of triangle. The diagram uses a shape to represent each of the three types of museums: a

Figure 2.1 This diagram shows the interplay between the three types of musuems. Destination musuems are represented by a circle, Curatoiral Musuems by a triangle, and Community musuems by a square. Museum Insights

circle for Destination (top), a square for Community (left), and a triangle for Curatorial (right). Over the years this diagram has become affectionately known as "the guitar pick diagram" (Figure 2.1). Because few museums are just circles, squares, or triangles, as the shapes move away from the points of the diagram, they begin to evolve, revealing how museums often incorporate aspects of at least two of the three types of museums. By shifting the shape's form and allowing it to take on aspects of a nearby shape, each of the three categories can be shown to make up a larger or smaller part of the museum's focus. Let's look at a few examples. A children's museum might be some form of square, or even the square in the corner because their hyper-focus is serving the community of families with young children in their region. The Rock & Roll Hall of Fame might be mostly circle-shaped, acknowledging its destination qualities, perhaps moving toward a triangle to represent its collecting role. An art museum at a university might be a triangle moving toward a square to reflect its curatorial work combined with its outreach role within the university community.

Looking at the guitar pick, it may be tempting to point to the center, where the categories converge, and conclude that the ideal museum would be at that blob-like shape. However, the adage, "you can't be all things to all people," also applies here. Museums that strive to be in the middle are continually pulled toward one corner or another, with no clear sense of their most important constituents or the unique ways the museum can meet their needs. As a result, museums that are striving to be everything to everyone fail to deliver enough of interest to any of their many different constituents, and often do not thrive.

Rather than striving to be all three types of museums, smack in the middle of the guitar pick, it is helpful to use the guitar pick to determine a museum's "center of gravity" and clarify the museum's primary constituents to bring the museum closest to fulfilling its mission. Defining a center of gravity does not stop the museum from conducting some activities more typical of other areas of the diagram. For example, most museums own and care for collections, but this alone does not make them a Curatorial Museum. And having a center of gravity located in a community or a destination does not mean the museum no longer cares for its collections or no longer actively collects. Instead, these

	Destination	Community	Curatorial
Primary Constituents	Constituents are primarily from out of town	Constituents are from the local community or are fans of your niche	Constituents are primarily scholars and researchers
Featured Activities	High-impact visitor experience	Wide variety of programs and changing exhibits	Focus is on collections, access, and research areas
Location & Architecture	Visible location and dramatic architecture	Accessibility is more important than visibility	Security is more important than access or visibility
Operating Funding	Dependent on earned income	Depends on earned and unearned income	Depends on government, institution, or endowment funding
Capital Funding	Periodic major capital infusions to update the visitor experience	Continual investment in programming. Constant reinvention	Infrequent major capital investments
Examples	Halls of fame, landmarks, and exceptional collections	History museums, children's museums, and local art museums	Research collections, university museums, and private collections
Outcomes	• Memories • Earned Revenue	• Engagement and Learning • Membership Revenue	• Deep knowledge • Endowment gifts

Figure 2.2 Operating Implications for Destination, Community, and Curatorial Museums. Museum Insights

activities are in service to the museum's community or destination role, rather than its primary reason for being, as they are in a Curatorial Museum. Figure 2.2 summarizes the operating and other implications of each type of museum. The following case studies show how these three distinct focuses are combined in practice.

CASE STUDY 1: THE ACADEMY MUSEUM OF MOTION PICTURES, LOS ANGELES, CALIFORNIA

The Academy Museum of Motion Pictures is a good example of a museum with both Destination and Community characteristics (Figure 2.3).[1]

Mission

The Academy Museum of Motion Pictures advances the understanding, celebration, and preservation of cinema through inclusive and accessible exhibitions, screenings, programs, initiatives, and collections.[2]

Primary Constituents

- Members of the film industry ranging from scholars and directors to camera operators, makeup artists, and others who make films happen (Regional Community)
- Film buffs (Affinity Community)
- Tourists to Los Angeles and Hollywood (Destination)

The Three Types of Museums

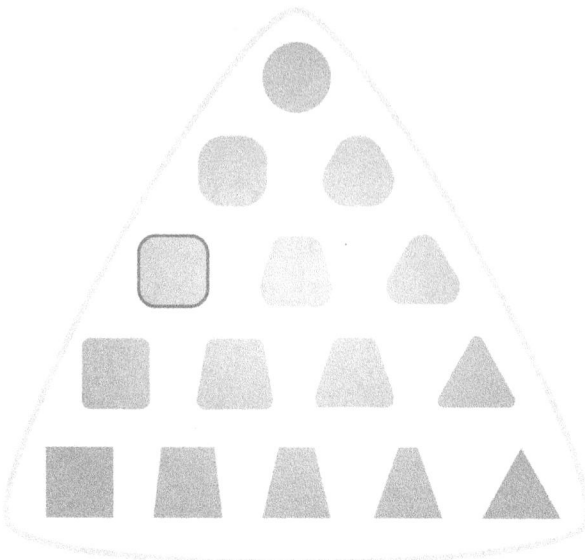

Figure 2.3 The Academy Museum of Motion Pictures is a good example of a museum with both Destination and Community characteristics. The shape with the dark outline in Figure 2.3 shows where it fits on the guitar pick diagram. Museum Insights

Primary Activities

The museum primary activities are its long-term and temporary exhibits, its film screenings, and its use as a special-event venue with state-of-the-art theaters and an event venue. The museum uses a renovated historic building for exhibits and programs designed for film enthusiasts and film professionals alike, including access to the Academy's film libraries and screenings of significant historic films as well as recent releases and material from up-and-coming directors or avant-garde filmmakers. A specifically designed one-thousand-seat theater and party space, an addition to the historic building, allows the museum to host movie premieres. The museum's film program and events spaces primarily support those working in the film industry today and film aficionados.[3] At the same time, the museum also recognizes its status as a tourist destination by offering special programs, like *The Oscars Experience*, which allows visitors to step up on a virtual stage, accept a real Oscar, make a speech (with the clock ticking down!), and take home a video documenting their moment on stage.[4] The Academy also has an extensive film library and a film industry archive, which are located and operated separately from the museum.[5]

Facilities

The museum contains two theaters, one of which was designed specifically for movie premieres. This building's roof deck, with views of the Hollywood sign in the Hollywood Hills, serves as a publicly accessible viewpoint for visitors by day and a setting for movie-premiere after-parties in the evenings. An upscale restaurant, in addition to other amenities, emphasizes that the museum is a gathering place for film community members as much as it serves destination visitors.[6]

Funding

While it is part of the Academy of Motion Picture Arts and Sciences, which is also responsible for the Oscar awards, given the museum's destination and community operations, it is likely that the museum is funded primarily with admissions revenue supplemented with memberships, donations, and support from the Academy.[7]

CASE STUDY 2: CENTER FOR PUPPETRY ARTS, ATLANTA, GEORGIA

The Center for Puppetry Arts is an example of a museum with both community and curatorial aspects (Figure 2.4).

Figure 2.4 The Center for Puppetry Arts is an example of a museum with both community and curatorial aspects. The shape with the dark outline in Figure 2.4 shows where it fits on the guitar pick diagram. Museum Insights

Mission

The Center for Puppetry Arts' mission is to inspire imagination, education, and community through the global art of puppetry.[8]

Primary Constituents

- Current and aspiring puppeteers seeking to see puppets in action and expand their skills (Affinity Community)
- Families with young children who want to watch puppet shows (Regional Community)
- Puppetry lovers (Affinity Community)
- Puppet and Jim Henson lovers who want to see exceptional puppets from around the world preserved and exhibited (Curatorial)

Primary Activities

The museum's activities fall into two primary categories: collecting and preserving significant puppets from around the world and showcasing the art of puppetry through performances and training opportunities for current and aspiring puppeteers. The museum's collection highlights puppets from all over the world and contains a gallery dedicated to pioneering puppeteer Jim Henson, who is best

The Three Types of Museums

remembered for his work with the Muppets and *Sesame Street*. The gallery showcases a re-creation of Henson's workshop and a large number of his puppets from projects spanning his career. A temporary gallery highlights contemporary puppets used in film, stage, and other productions. In total, these galleries emphasize that puppetry is an ancient art practiced around the world, and it has a strong impact on cultures past and present. The rest of the museum's building is given over to a theater for live puppetry and space for training future puppeteers. A packed schedule of performances designed for both families with children during the day and adults after dark brings the wonder of puppetry to a variety of audiences.[9]

Facility

Located in a repurposed school in Atlanta's Midtown neighborhood, the bright-green building is easy to find, with plentiful parking and access via public transit. Inside, accessibility for all, with special thought given to strollers and the needs of families, makes sure community members feel at home in this regional destination.[10]

Finances

Most of the Center's income comes from donations, with program service revenue (here, including its robust workshop and puppet show offerings) a close second.[11]

CASE STUDY 3: THE ART COMPLEX MUSEUM, DUXBURY, MASSACHUSETTS

The Art Complex Museum is a strong example of a Community Museum (figure 2.5).

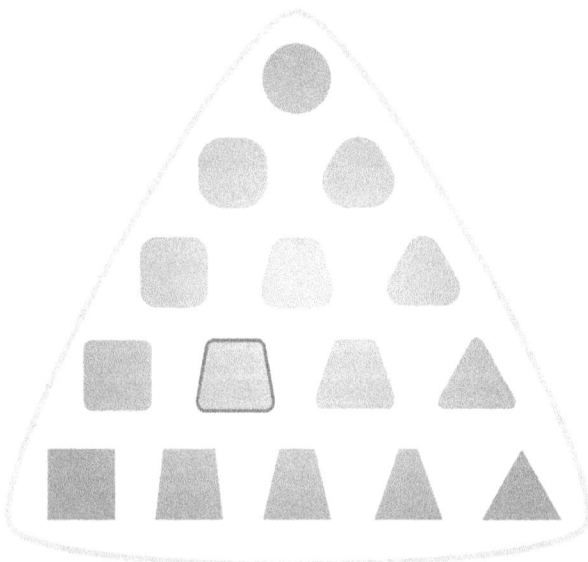

Figure 2.5 The Art Complex Museum is a strong example of a Community Museum. The shape with the dark outline in Figure 2.5 shows where it fits on the guitar pick diagram. Museum Insights

Mission

The Art Complex Museum serves as a regional art center and houses the impressive collection of the Carl A. Weyerhaeuser family. The museum offers a year-round schedule of exhibitions, lectures, concerts, classes, education programs, demonstrations, and tea ceremonies fulfilling the founders' vision that their family's many interests be shared with the community.[12]

Primary Constituents

- Regional art lovers (Community)
- Regional contemporary artists (Community)
- Aficionados of the museum's unique collections, such as Shaker furniture (Affinity Community)

Primary Activities

The Art Complex Museum devotes its two main galleries to exhibits from contemporary artists working in New England, especially the Greater Boston area. Two smaller galleries hold rotating exhibits that feature pieces from the founders' diverse collection. Like many family museums, the museum's collections are eclectic, but focused on a few key areas. The major strengths of the collection are American paintings; Shaker furniture and artifacts; and works on paper, the majority of which are American and European prints. Also of great significance is the Asian art collection. A small temporary gallery allows the museum to mount temporary exhibits from the collection, along with the two larger galleries that primarily focus on contemporary art. A full programming schedule, including gallery talks, art workshops, tea ceremonies at the museum's tea hut, and musical performances, makes the museum a lively gathering place for the arts on Boston's south shore.[13]

Facility

The museum's iconic wave-like roof evokes the ocean and draws natural light into the building. Built into a hill, the museum allows visitors enter the primary gallery and program spaces on the first floor, which overlooks a pond. Curatorial functions take place on the lower level, while an adjacent, repurposed house serves as a studio for art workshops and classes.[14]

Finances

The Art Complex Museum is fully funded by the Weyerhaeuser family as a gift to the community.[15]

The first chapters have laid out the theoretical underpinnings of the museum master planning process. Now it's time to get to work. The next chapter will outline the practical foundations needed for a successful planning process, including how to assemble a planning team and assess where your museum is now. In the chapters that follow, we will outline the planning process with templates, sample documents, and other tools to help start the process at your museum.

NOTES

1. Please note: This, and other case studies in this section, are based on the authors' analysis from outside the museum and may or may not reflect the museum's own understanding of their constituents and related activities and programs.

2. Academy Museum of Motion Pictures, "About," Academy Museum of Motion Pictures, https://www.academymuseum.org/en/about (accessed October 11, 2023).
3. Academy Museum of Motion Pictures, "Public Programs," Academy Museum of Motion Pictures, https://www.academymuseum.org/en/programs/section/public-programs (accessed October 11, 2023).
4. Academy Museum of Motion Pictures, "The Oscars Experience," Academy Museum of Motion Pictures, https://www.academymuseum.org/en/exhibitions/oscars-experience (accessed October 11, 2023).
5. Academy of Motion Picture Arts and Sciences, "Margaret Herrick Library," Academy of Motion Picture Arts and Sciences, https://www.oscars.org/library (accessed October 11, 2023).
6. Academy Museum of Motion Pictures, "About," Academy Museum of Motion Pictures, https://www.academymuseum.org/en/about (accessed October 11, 2023). Guy Hermann also completed initial planning work for this museum and is familiar with the design concepts.
7. As the museum operates as part of the Academy of Motion Picture Arts and Sciences, its specific finances are difficult to draw out from the Academy's public 990 filings.
8. Center for Puppetry Arts, "Our Mission and History," Center for Puppetry Arts, https://puppet.org/about/ (accessed October 12, 2023).
9. Center for Puppetry Arts, "Programs," Center for Puppetry Arts, https://puppet.org/programs/ (accessed October 12, 2023).
10. Center for Puppetry Arts, "History of Center for Puppetry Arts," Center for Puppetry Arts, https://puppet.org/history/ (accessed October 12, 2023). The authors' visit in April 2023 also informed this section.
11. Center for Puppetry Arts, Inc., "Center for Puppetry Arts Inc.," ProPublica Nonprofit Explorer, https://projects.propublica.org/nonprofits/organizations/581275610 (accessed October 12, 2023).
12. Art Complex Museum, "About the Art Complex Museum," Art Complex Museum, https://artcomplex.org/about/ (accessed October 11, 2023).
13. Art Complex Museum, "Programs," Art Complex Museum, https://artcomplex.org/programs/ (accessed October 11, 2023).
14. Art Complex Museum, "History of the Art Complex Museum," Art Complex Museum, https://artcomplex.org/about/history/ (accessed October 11, 2023). The authors also completed facilities planning for this museum and drew on their personal knowledge.
15. The Art Complex Museum operates as a private foundation. Art Complex Inc., "Art Complex Inc.," ProPublica Nonprofit Explorer, https://projects.propublica.org/nonprofits/organizations/46155696/202233189349104988/IRS990PF (accessed October 11, 2023).

3

The Practical Foundations of Master Planning

Beyond the theoretical foundations outlined in the opening chapters, it is also important to develop practical foundations for a master planning effort before launching the process. In this chapter, we will outline the research and actions you need to take to get the most out of the planning process that follows.

DEVELOPING A PLANNING TEAM

A successful planning process is never a solo endeavor. Successful planning takes time to listen to all the voices in the room (and outside the room). A critical starting point is assembling a planning team of five to seven people. A good planning team uses a variety of approaches and methods to engage all of the museum's stakeholders in meaningful ways. The team should be large enough to have differences of opinion, and small enough to be able to resolve these differences amicably. Team members should be excited about the process and prepared to commit to six to twelve months of regular meetings, punctuated with time for analysis and reflection. When assembling the planning team, seek to bring several different perspectives from the staff and board, being sure to include both newcomers and old-timers and individuals interested in different museum focus areas or departments. The mix of people is often more important than a single person's position or title. Board members may have more experience with large-scale planning; staff members will have a better understanding of museums in general. Typically, executive leadership is represented by the museum's director and the board (or the board's planning committee) chair. Other members of the board and staff should be added based on their skills; attributes, such as donor or influencer; and propensity for thinking critically about the future. The planning team becomes the group that will serve as emissaries for the plan once they complete the planning process. Be sure that members can fulfill both the planning and sharing aspects of the role when selecting members.

BACKGROUND RESEARCH

Before starting to plan, the planning team needs to take a deep dive into the museum's history and operations to know where the museum has been, to understand its current position, and to internalize any planning work accomplished previously. By completing this research, or as it is known in consulting, "discovery," all members of the planning team start with a similar knowledge base. This matters. While a board member on the finance committee may have a good grasp of the museum's expenditures, the curator may not. Likewise, a staff member focused on public programming may not understand the museum's curatorial policies, and so on. To develop this shared knowledge base, it is necessary to put together a package of materials documenting prior planning work, current operations, and documentation of the museum's site and existing buildings, if any. While being comprehensive is important, it is also important to be thoughtful about the capacity of the planning team to review information. The goal is to develop a shared knowledge base, not to suffer from information overload. While it is usually better to err on the side of too much information—one never knows where the kernel of a transformative idea might be hiding—it is also pointless to provide additional information if it will not be reviewed by the planning team. Below is a list of suggested materials that all members of the planning team should review. This list should be adapted based on the specific circumstances of your museum.

- Prior studies and planning work, such as strategic plans, long-range plans, development of mission statements, and so on.
- Interpretive plans.
- Exhibit plans and/or public programming plans.
- Floor plans, site plans, and landscape plans.
- Scope of Collections statement or collection policy documents.
- History of the organization.
- Legal agreements such as MOUs with partner organizations.
- Financial statements.
- Lists of any legally binding obligations (agreements with governments, bequest restrictions, etc.).
- Any other resources or documentation that might be helpful to the planning team.

Once the team has reviewed the document package, they should convene to discuss any questions or reactions from the review. At the conclusion of this review or discovery period, each member of the team should feel firmly grounded in the museum's past and current operations. The next step will be to use this shared understanding to assess the museum's resources, constraints, opportunities, and challenges.

PRELIMINARY ASSESSMENT: RESOURCES, CONSTRAINTS, OPPORTUNITIES, AND CHALLENGES

Critical to the success of any planning process is understanding the landscape in which the museum operates. The next step for the planning team is to conduct a preliminary assessment of the museum to answer some of the following questions: Whom do you currently serve? Why them? Who are your current partners? Why them? What are the areas where your organization is thriving? What is working? What isn't? Where are the significant opportunities for the future? One way to draw these many threads together is to develop a framework focusing on the museum's Resources, Constraints, Challenges, and Opportunities. This framework can bring the current organization into focus and help to understand its potential future.

- *Resources* are things the organization has that will help move it forward. They may be tangible things, like exhibits, collections, funding sources, buildings, and people, or they may be more intangible things, like community support, a capable board, or a visionary director.
- *Constraints* are the things that are unlikely to ever change. These could include restrictions on a particular collection or fund, specific attributes of an organization's location, the missions and services of similar organizations in your area, property restrictions, and governmental regulations. For most organizations, the list of constraints will be short. True constraints are immovable

obstacles. Perhaps most important, constraints are likely battles not worth fighting. Trying to change where change is unlikely can sap an organization's energy and divide its supporters.
- *Challenges* represent things that are hard or difficult for the museum to change, but that could be changed with sustained effort. Examples of challenges include a building that does not meet current programmatic needs, departments that are understaffed, an out-of-date organizational mission, or the need for additional operating funds. It is important to distinguish between challenges and constraints to focus resources and attention where they can be most effective.
- *Opportunities* are areas where the organization can meet its mission in new or expanded ways. Opportunities may include serving current constituents differently or reaching out to new constituent groups. Opportunities can also be something more concrete, like acquiring a significant collection or finding a new funding source, designing a new building, or renovating an old one. From a master planning perspective, opportunities have the power to change the organization and expand its constituencies as part of multiyear initiatives or a purposeful repositioning of the organization.

Developing a list of Resources, Constraints, Challenges, and Opportunities should be one of the planning team's first tasks. Note that the purpose of this exercise is not to make decisions about reallocating resources or seizing new opportunities. This work helps to identify the threads of possibility that run through the museum that can be developed long-term to keep your museum providing the services that engage, inspire, and challenge your constituents. Initially, it is worthwhile to include everything that comes to mind in each category. Encourage the planning team to think broadly, to be attuned to both positive and negative factors affecting the museum, and to be open-minded about potential opportunities. Generally, opportunities are not things you are already doing. They require significant changes to a current activity or taking a risk by offering something new that will serve the needs of your constituents in new ways. Even an idea that isn't fully realized and may have hidden constraints or that requires taking significant risks is worth noting as an opportunity. Striving to grow the museum in new ways, even if it is already successful, is how your museum will stay vital to those whom you serve now and into the future. When identifying opportunities to pursue, it is wise to give them a quick check against the list of constraints. Rarely is it worth pursuing an opportunity if it conflicts with a known constraint. A sample list of Resources, Constraints, Challenges, and Opportunities is provided as Resource 3.1.

As the planning team develops the list of Resources, Constraints, Challenges and Opportunities, it may become apparent that there some specific issues, difficulties, or concerns that planning team members already understand and want to see specifically acknowledged at this point in the planning process. A tool for addressing these is to create a list called "Issues and Concerns." This list names a particular problem and provides a brief explanation as to why it is a problem. For example, the team might identify parking as a concern, stating, "the museum's parking lot is not large enough to accommodate the current level of visitation, especially on rainy days or for popular programs. The limited parking severely compromises the museum's ability to host larger events because they require additional, off-site parking which requires a shuttle, which is expensive for the museum and often unpopular with attendees." At this point, the purpose is to identify problems, not to determine solutions. There is more planning work that needs to be done before the committee can clearly see the possible solutions and consider which solution provides the most overall benefit to the museum.

The work to develop Resources, Constraints, Challenges, and Opportunities, along with Issues and Concerns may lead some members more experienced with planning to ask, why not a Strengths, Weaknesses, Opportunities, and Threats (SWOT) framework? While this approach shares some aspects of a traditional SWOT framework, this alternate framework has some important differences. The key difference is that SWOT is primarily a decision-making or strategic planning tool.[1] As referenced in the University of Kansas Community Toolbox, the "purpose of performing a SWOT is

The Practical Foundations of Master Planning

to reveal positive forces that work together and potential problems that need to be recognized and possibly addressed." That is, conducting a SWOT should provide an informed baseline of where your organization is right now, which can help you assess the risks and benefits of different decision-making paths. When thinking long-term, as is the goal of this book, we need to think about overcoming more challenging weaknesses and taking advantage of more comprehensive opportunities.

The Resources, Constraints, Challenges, and Opportunities analysis serves as an initial set of guardrails for the planning process by steering planning away from things that are not feasible and toward the opportunities available. Resources lead to opportunities. Opportunities are shaped by mission and vision and are limited by constraints and challenges. The document may be revised as the planning process continues and new information becomes available. One important time to review this document again is following the constituent interviews, described in chapter 5. Depending on how the museum's planning process evolves, revisiting the Resources, Constraints, Challenges, and Opportunities may be useful at other junctures as well.

Before reading further, take a few minutes to think about your own museum. What are some of the museums and organizations that you consider your peers or your competitors? Benchmarking is a critical step in the master planning process, as it can help pull aside the curtain to reveal how other museums actually operate. Perhaps most important, benchmarking helps the planning team to see through the carefully curated veneers of a wide variety of museums and determine the many different ways that museums can be successful. In the next chapter, we will explore how to conduct a benchmarking exercise.

A NOTE ON DIVERSITY, EQUITY, ACCESSIBILITY, AND INCLUSION (DEAI)

Over the last decade, calls for the museum field to reflect on inequity within their institutions have become increasingly widespread.[2] Many have noted that inequities were, and are, pervasive—apparent in what the museum collected, what it chose to exhibit, whom it encouraged to visit, whom it hired, and how it compensated and treated its staff, interns, and volunteers. These calls coalesced around the concept of DEAI (Diversity, Equity, Accessibility, and Inclusion). Calls for active DEAI work increased in 2020, following the murder of George Floyd and the COVID-19 pandemic, which exposed and exacerbated existing challenges. Many museums pledged to begin or increase DEAI work.[3] At the time of this book's publication [2025], conversations about DEAI remained active, and practices continue to evolve. Still, there is consensus that DEAI work is most effective when it is an ongoing process. There must be a commitment to reflection and action by both the institution and its staff, board, and volunteers. DEAI is most successful when it is woven into every department and aspect of the museum's operations, not as an independent pillar or a responsibility of one department. It is not a one-and-done checkbox; as the museum makes progress, DEAI work must also develop new practices and set new goals to embed DEAI into the culture of the organization.[4]

Wherever your museum is in the process of DEAI work, we encourage you to review your most recent DEAI road maps and goals at the start of this planning work and to weave them into the long-term vision you and the planning team are developing for your museum through the exercises in this book. We hope that this master planning process can be one more tool to help your museum integrate your DEAI practices into current and future operations. At certain points in this book, we will suggest checking in with the museum's DEAI work. Of course, these check-ins may not align with where your museum is in your DEAI process. Feel free to disregard those that don't fit and add in DEAI elements to the planning process as they reflect your museum's process and progress toward your DEAI goals.

RESOURCE 3.1: SAMPLE RESOURCES, CONSTRAINTS, CHALLENGES, AND OPPORTUNITIES SUMMARY

Resources

- A beautiful location with stunning views
- Staff skilled in developing engaging exhibits
- Potential significant donors
- A reputation for showing up and following through

Constraints

- Limits on developing the property due to abutting properties
- Zoning and other legal constraints on the use of the property
- The housing crisis and its effect on finding qualified staff

Challenges

- Uncatalogued collections
- Lack of name recognition for the organization
- Awkward exhibit spaces
- Inadequate parking

Opportunities

- Food and drink on the grounds in the evening
- A role as the area's flagship museum
- A special role to play in school-age programming
- Potential to be a strong, year-round cultural resource
- Making arts more central with potential new partnerships

NOTES

1. Community Tool Box Team, "Section 14. SWOT Analysis: Strengths, Weaknesses, Opportunities, and Threats," University of Kansas Center for Community Health and Development, https://ctb.ku.edu/en/table-of-contents/assessment/assessing-community-needs-and-resources/swot-analysis/main#:~:text=What%20are%20the%20elements%20of,be%20recognized%20and%20possibly%20addressed (accessed October 11, 2023).
2. American Alliance of Museums, "Excellence in DEAI," American Alliance of Museums, https://www.aam-us.org/wp-content/uploads/2022/07/AAM-Excellence-in-DEAI-Report.pdf (accessed August 9, 2024).
3. Cecilia Garibay and Jeanne Marie Olson, "CCLI National Landscape Study: The State of DEAI Practices in Museums," Cultural Competence Learning Institute, https://higherlogicdownload.s3.amazonaws.com/ASTC/a6c0f3de-e0b1-4198-8ab7-01cee4a55b00/UploadedImages/CCLI_National_Landscape_Study-DEAI_Practices_in_Museums_2020.pdf (accessed August 9, 2024).
4. See, for example, the section titled "Equity" in Avi Y. Decter, Marsha L. Semmel, and Ken Yellis, *Change Is Required: Preparing for the Post-Pandemic Museum* (Lanham, MD: Rowman & Littlefield, 2022).

4

Benchmarking
Learning from Others' Success

Benchmarking gives the planning team the chance to take a deep dive into the many interesting and unusual ways that other museums have succeeded. Studying how others have addressed similar challenges builds an understanding of possible paths a museum could take to meet its own goals. Benchmarking provides two key outcomes. First, it helps a museum see the variety of ways that other similar organizations have overcome obstacles or embraced similar opportunities or constraints. Second, it provides a menu of solutions from which your museum can begin to develop a viable master plan unique to the needs of your institution. No less important, benchmarking can be fun! It is a chance to dive into other museums' operations and programs and, depending on the financial resources of your organization, an opportunity to travel to other museums and meet other staff doing similar work. Benchmarking opens the planning team's eyes to the wide variety of ways that museums address challenges, likely including some identified in earlier stages of your own planning process. Perhaps most important, benchmarking helps the planning team to develop a shared understanding of the realities of museum operations. This chapter provides an overview of the benchmarking process, step-by-step guides to help you complete the process at your museum, and recommendations for how to analyze the information you gather.

PICKING INSTITUTIONS TO BENCHMARK

The overarching reason to benchmark another institution is to understand how their solutions can be adapted to become part of your museum's operations and strategy. Benchmark museums can be selected for a variety of reasons. Below, we've outlined some of the common categories we use to develop a list of organizations to benchmark and the ways that each organization is effective. Keep in mind that not all categories will yield important information for your museum's planning project. Consider your main goals and desired outcomes from the planning. What do you expect will change? How will you shift your museum's direction or focus? How have others addressed similar issues? For example, if expanding education programs for students in grades K–5 is not a goal of the planning process, then focusing on museums with effective K–5 education programs does not provide the information that will help make changes. On the other hand, if developing a new building or addition with green technologies or making an old building more efficient in both space use and energy use is a priority, then benchmarking museums who have recently gone through this process will be illuminating. As you review the categories below, focus on the questions that will provide information useful to your unique needs.

Similar Constituencies

Museums that primarily serve constituent groups similar to the groups that you plan to serve make excellent benchmarks. Note that identifying the constituents you expect to serve is distinct from identifying the museum's subject matter. For example, a history museum, an art museum, and a science center might all serve third graders. While the content might differ, there will likely be similarities in how each museum meets the needs of this distinct constituent group. Therefore, when benchmarking based on constituencies served, it is important to consider a wide range of other organizations. A science museum might offer important lessons on connecting with youth that can be translated to a historic house; a historic house's successful volunteer program could help an art museum strengthen engagement with their community; and a children's museum's focus on play and discovery could enliven the work of a nature center. When you see another organization successfully serving one of your constituencies, think about how their methods could be adapted to work within the bounds of your museum. This category is used for all types of museums.

Similar Subject Matter

Most museums begin the benchmarking process by identifying museums with similar subject matter. Museums or other organizations that share your themes can suggest different ways of presenting similar material, connecting with your constituents, and developing an operational model, even if they operate in different geographic contexts. For example, the home of a famous writer would benchmark other homes or museums dedicated to the work of other famous authors. This category is useful for all types of museums, but it is limited if it is the primary criteria.

Similar Size

Museums that are roughly the same size as yours likely have similar operations and challenges. "Size" in this context can reference physical space, staff size, collection size, budget, or other factors you determine to be of interest. For example, if a goal is to increase public programs, examining the number of program staff at a museum doing programming you find worth emulating could provide insights into how staffing levels might need to adjust to accommodate more public programs at your museum. If you are comparing programs, also be sure to consider the size of the museum's budget compared to yours, as well as the physical space they have available to make sure it is a reasonable comparison. Benchmarking similar-sized museums is useful for all types of museums.

Similar Region or Geographic Area

Understanding other museums and similar organizations operating in your geographic area often provides a way to understand how your museum fits in the region's broader cultural context and the kinds of roles and activities you could take on that aren't being provided by any other organization. Regional organizations are also operating within the same pool of potential donors and visitors as your museum. Benchmarking nearby museums can also show you where the most promising opportunities are. Even if an opportunity looks like something your museum could do well, it's unlikely to succeed if another organization is already doing something similar. For example, if several museums in your region already provide well-regarded early childhood programs, there may not be space in the market for a similar, new program at your museum. Therefore, it might be more prudent to pursue a different set of constituents. This category of benchmarks is particularly important for museums whose primary focus is community.

Notable Programming

A museum or organization may be of interest for benchmarking because of a notable program or event that particularly speaks to your constituents or aspirations. Examples of notable programs include a successful, sustained community curation program, an outreach program that engaged a new constituency with the museum, a festival or event that drew together communities of interest, or high-quality education programs serving students inside and outside the classroom. This category is most useful for Community Museums, including those that also have destination characteristics.

Notable Museums

This category includes museums that everyone knows or that staff and/or board members find especially impressive, engaging, or otherwise worth emulating. Identifying the kinds of programs, facilities, and operating models that are exciting or appealing to staff and board members and including some aspects of them into the long-range plan can improve buy-in and willingness to implement change. Care must be taken here to fully understand the financial model underpinning the museum. Often, notable museums have significant endowments or active donors that underpin programming. Understanding the financial models for notable museums can also be useful in explaining to board members why your museum is unable to produce the same caliber of work without significant change or investment. This category is useful for all types of museums.

Peer Museums or Organizations

This category often overlaps with the topic and size categories outlined above. Simply put, when you think about institutions you could consider your peer or doing very similar work (whether close to home or on another continent), what are they? These museums should be added to the list even if you are seeking to change how your museum operates because these peers (or museums you would like to be your peers) are an important starting place for understanding challenges and areas of success. This category is useful for all types of museums.

Unusual Shared Characteristics

Some museums may have characteristics that are not easy to capture. For example, a planning project for a small art museum funded by a family foundation led us to benchmark museums run by family foundations. Using that characteristic proved to be very useful to understand business models that were distinct from typical nonprofits. This category may be useful to museums of any type that have a distinct characteristic that sets apart their mission or operations.

Museum Failures

Looking at museums that have failed or are struggling can be a useful exercise because it identifies solutions that are unlikely to work. One example of a project that included benchmarking failures was a local industrial history museum that was offered a significant collection of political memorabilia related to both local and national politics. The offer came with funds to help develop a new building that would also better accommodate the museum's industrial collections. The board was divided, as the collection was not within their focus area, but taking it could dramatically improve the display of their primary artifacts. The donor was certain that the collection would draw many new visitors from the community and beyond. Benchmarking museums of political memorabilia revealed that while there is a lively community of memorabilia collectors, the museums that only focused on political memorabilia did not support themselves from earned revenue linked to visitation. Two such collections that had opened to the public had since closed. The lesson learned is that the passion of the collector may not reflect the interests and needs of the museum's constituents, and this gave the board important data as they considered accepting the collection. Still, we do not typically recommend benchmarking failures unless your museum is in a situation like this one and can benefit from testing the possibility presented against the realities other organizations have encountered.

MAKING THE INITIAL LIST

For some museums, drafting a list of museums and other organizations to benchmark will be very straightforward. Historic house museums, community art museums, nature centers, children's museums, and others share many common attributes. Identifying exemplary organizations to benchmark in these areas should not be difficult. It is more challenging when your organization crosses the typical boundaries—the historic house museum that has a significant art collection, the public garden taking on an environmental mission, the history museum that celebrates the work of a prominent scientist, or that special family museum that hasn't changed a thing since it opened seventy-five years ago. The trick is to identify organizations with attributes you would like to emulate, even if that is only part of what they do. If a museum's public programs are exemplary, and that is one focus of yours, put them on the list. If a museum has devised a better way for visitors to engage with collections, and that is another focus for your museum, put them on the list. If yours is a straightforward project, your list may be short, with four or five museums to learn from. If you have multiple areas of growth and change, you will likely have several lists, each focusing on a different set of museums serving different constituencies.

Once you have identified museums and other organizations to benchmark, you need to identify the kinds of information you want to learn about each one. Generally, you should research the same information about every museum on the list so that your understanding of each is relatively equal. If there is a particular aspect of operations that you want to interrogate more closely that is not present at other museums, that's okay, too, as long as the difference is clear. In general, the research should begin by answering three overarching questions:

- Whom do they serve? What is their mission?
- What are the activities they undertake to fulfill the mission?
- Why do they matter? What experiences or practices at this museum are applicable to your institution?

Your goal at the end of your research is to be able to answer each of these questions in a sentence or two to provide a quick and digestible overview to other members of the planning team and to spark discussion about what aspects of each benchmark may be useful to emulate or which parts of the data you've gathered is worth digging into further.

Once the big picture is clear, work to more fully understand the other museum's operations. Depending on the focus of your project, you may want to gather data for some or all of the following areas:

- Mission and vision
- Primary constituent groups
- Annual visitation
- Entry fees
- Membership programs
- Notable education and school programs

- Notable public programs
- Notable partnerships or sponsorships
- Size of staff/concentration of staffing (programs, curatorial, etc.)
- Size/scope of collections
- Size of building, nature of facilities
- Staff size and allocation of positions
- Location (rural, urban, etc.)
- Financials: breakdown of income and expenses; operating at a surplus or loss

This list may seem daunting, but most of the information can be pulled from three publicly available sources: the museum's website, the museum's annual report, and its 990 federal tax reports. Questions about mission, entry fees, notable education/public programs, unusual partnerships, location, partnerships, and staff can usually be found on the museum's website. Most museums also post their annual reports, which can provide detailed information about changing exhibits, programs, visitation, and special activities. In the Putting It All Together section, we will provide tables to track and compare the information you are gathering.

If you have trouble finding the information you need, you may want to reach out to a member of the museum's staff. We have found museum staffers universally willing to help (people love to talk about their museums), but it is still best to be thoughtful as to how you approach the other museum. Not all institutions may be comfortable disclosing visitation or financial information beyond what is available in an annual report or a 990 form. Likewise, most museums will be more comfortable discussing successes—reach out very gently to talk about any failures. Finally, try to target your request to the person most likely to have the answers. Questions about a specific program are likely best directed to the program director or education lead; questions about operations or funding to the director or deputy director; and collection-specific questions to the curator. Offer individuals the opportunity for a phone call or to respond to specific questions in writing depending on their preference. Either way, be respectful of their time by keeping your list of questions as short and focused as possible, and a thank-you afterward is always welcome. A recommended list of questions is provided as Resource 4.1. In some cases, an actual visit to other museums may be useful, especially if your research has turned up unexpected results. Reading the website and online reviews seldom gives the full story. If you do plan a visit, it is best if the entire planning team can travel together as team members will see the museum from their own perspectives. Do reach out to the other museums ahead of your visit and be sure to get behind the scenes where the challenges most likely lie.

GATHERING COMPARABLE FINANCIAL DATA

The easiest way to gain an initial understanding of a benchmarked museum's financial position is through their IRS Form 990, the publicly available form required by the IRS of all nonprofit organizations. The 990 forms are available for free online through ProPublica, GuideStar, and other resources. While 990 forms can look daunting, for the purposes of benchmarking, the key information can be found on the first page of the form. (We recommend recording the following data in Template 4.1.) To keep things consistent when looking up 990s, be sure to use the same filing year for each organization.

First, record the total revenue and the value for each of the primary categories defined by the IRS:

- Contributions and grants (money given to an organization by donors or money granted to an organization by a nonprofit, foundation, or government)
- Program service revenue (money earned from programs or services provided by the organization; in museums this is often program fees, gift shop revenue, and event rental fees)

- Investment income (typically money from an endowment)
- Other revenue (revenue that does not fit into the above categories)

The goal here is to determine how the museum receives most of its money: Do they rely on donations? What percentage of revenue is earned? How robust is the museum's endowment, if any? This initial scan can provide valuable information about whether this is a good benchmark. If the benchmarked museum has a substantial endowment and your museum relies primarily on annual donations, your program and business models may be substantially different. Museums with similar revenue sources are likely the best benchmarks, unless, of course, you are considering a major change to the way you operate. After reviewing the revenue numbers on the cover page, it is also worth taking a look at part eight of Form 990, which breaks down revenue sources in greater detail. This can reveal things like museum store income versus program income and so on. If these details seem significant, note them.[1]

Next, look at the expenses section on the cover page, noting total expenses and the value for each expense category:

- Grants and similar amounts paid (grants made by the organization to others)
- Benefits paid to or for members (usually zero for most museums)
- Salaries, other compensation, employee benefits
- Professional fundraising fees
- Other expenses

This time, the purpose is to understand where the money goes. For most museums, salaries and benefits will be the most significant expense, typically 50 to 60 percent of operating costs. Beyond that, costs vary with the specifics of each museum's programming and funding sources. For example, it would be reasonable for a museum that relies heavily on donations to have an active series of programs and more significant fundraising costs. If any of the numbers seem unexpectedly large or small in comparison to others, you can review Form 990 part nine, which provides a breakout of the expense categories in more detail. Your intention here is *not* an exercise in forensic accounting. It is to gain a broad understanding of where the money goes in relation to how the museum operates. That is, to operate as this museum does, how is money allocated? If your museum were to operate in a similar fashion, would its expenses need to be reallocated, too?

Next, you will see if the organization is operating with a surplus or a loss, or if it is merely breaking even. If the report shows a large surplus or loss, it is worth looking at 990 reports before and after the one you are reviewing. This can help you determine the direction things are going. For example, one year of loss could represent an investment in the future, such as the purchase of property, or an unexpected circumstance, such as the failure of mechanical systems or a disaster event. Likewise, one year of surplus could represent a onetime sale of property or another financial windfall, or it might simply be sound fiscal management. If there is a pattern of losses, it may suggest that an organization is facing challenges or undergoing change.

As you look at 990s, it is also important to recognize the impacts of COVID-19. The virus had immediate impacts on many museum bottom lines, both positively (with government support and grants for cultural organizations) and negatively (through lost revenue and visitation). Similarly, many organizations reconsidered their operating and program models as COVID restrictions ended. Older forms may not be indicative of a museum's current financial position and operating model. The 990 forms for the years 2019 to 2022 are unlikely to reflect current operations. Forms from 2023 forward should be indicative of a museum's "new normal." Remember that 990s are only one tool for understanding an organization's financial position—take into consideration other information you've learned from annual reports and other sources as you draw conclusions.

PUTTING IT ALL TOGETHER

Research complete, start to work with the information you've gathered. We have found it helpful to compile a short narrative summary and to also compile information into a series of tables. The following templates provide one way to organize the data you've gathered about the organization's financials, entry fees, attendance, and staffing.

- Template 4.1: Financials
- Template 4.2: Annual attendance, entry fees, and membership
- Template 4.3: Staffing, size, and location

Template 4.1 Museum Financials Tracking Table

	Museum A	Museum B	Museum C
Revenue			
Contributions and Grants			
Program Service Revenue			
Investment Income			
Other			
Total			
Expenses			
Grants and Similar Amounts Paid			
Benefits to or for Members			
Salaries, Other Compensation, Employee Benefits			
Professional Fundraising Fees			
Other Expenses			
Total			
Revenue Minus Expenses			
Notes			

Template 4.2 Museum Attendance and Entry Fee Tracking Table

	Museum A	Museum B	Museum C
Total Annual Attendance			
Entry Fee			
Membership Fees			
Notes			

Template 4.3 Museum Staffing and Facility Tracking Table

	Museum A	Museum B	Museum C
Total Full-Time Staff			
Total Part-Time Staff			
Total FTEs			
Total Volunteers			
Facility Size (Square Feet)			
Location (Urban, Rural, Suburban, etc.)			

With the data in tables, you can start to see some patterns. For example: Do most of the museums you benchmarked charge fees? What's the range in visitation? How big is the museum? How is space allocated? How much does the endowment contribute to annual operations? How big is the local community? When you see a pattern, make a note of it.

While financial and other data may be easier to compile and important to understand, the programmatic and operational lessons and big ideas may be more useful, and more inspiring. We recommend listing these lessons and ideas separately for each benchmarked museum while again looking for patterns. What worked? Why does it work? Would it work at your museum? For example, if several museums have successful programming for teens, what else do they have in common? Does your museum have similar building blocks? What might it take to develop similar programming at your museum?

Compile all this information in a benchmark report for the planning committee to review. This can take many forms, ranging from a fully-fleshed-out narrative to a slide deck that hits the high points and focuses on the lessons learned. A simple approach is to begin with a short introduction describing the main lessons learned from the process and then provide a list of all the benchmarked sites with the three big questions answered. Add pertinent details, like the primary lessons learned for each site. Following this overview, add in your tables, qualitative summaries or notes, and any other backup data that committee members might want to review more closely. Usually, it is best to keep this preliminary analysis short and simple, with key takeaways clearly stated and easily digested by the planning team and, ultimately, board members.

The planning committee should use the benchmarking exercise to inform the planning process in several ways. First, the process injects new ideas and possibilities into the process, which can help if some stakeholders are already set on one outcome or approach. The proven success of the benchmark sites may offer some risk mitigation as you move forward. Second, lessons learned through benchmarking can become a rough draft of where you are going by gathering ideas or activities that you may want to make part of your plan and what you might want to avoid. Benchmarking can give you the first rough estimates of the kinds of funding, space, staffing, and activities that you will need to offer if you want to emulate a particular aspect of another museum's operations. Finally, benchmarking offers a chance to examine your goals and ideas from a different perspective. If, in reviewing the benchmarks, you find outcomes that are unappealing, then perhaps the proposed changes should be revisited.

CASE STUDIES

A literary museum connected to a university offers an interesting example of the variety of museums and cultural centers that can shed light on a museum's operations. For this museum, we benchmarked a wide range of museums, libraries, and cultural centers, which included the following categories:

- Literary Historic House Museums, like the Mark Twain Boyhood Home (Hannibal, MO) and the Laura Ingalls Wilder Home (Independence, KS)
- Historic House Museums with a cultural focus like the Thomas Cole National Historic Site (Catskill, NY) and The Mount (Lenox, MA)
- Community-Engaged or Activist Museums, like the Wren's Nest (Atlanta, GA) and the Harriet Beecher Stowe Center (Hartford, CT)
- Academic and Research Centers, like the Folger Shakespeare Library (Washington, DC) and the Center for Ray Bradbury Studies (Indiana University-Purdue University of Indianapolis)
- Independent Literary Centers and Libraries, like the Rosenbach Library (Philadelphia, PA) and the National Steinbeck Center (Salinas, CA)
- Literary sites linked to colleges and universities, like Robert Frost's Stone House (Bennington College, Bennington, VT) and William Faulker's Rowan Oak (University of Mississippi, Oxford)

For this museum, the benchmarks provided a wide array of possible operating models that aligned with areas of interest for the board and staff. The benchmark report provided useful information that helped the museum decide to focus first on becoming a better literary historic house museum while also deepening its outreach to students and inspiring creative expression at the site. They reserved their aspiration to become a research center as a long-term goal.

While benchmarks are extremely valuable for most planning projects, sometimes they are not well received. One example is a historical society in a small city that was seeking to better represent the city's diversity. The society owned a historic house but did not use it for exhibits and were hesitant to use it for programs because the house was not ADA-compliant, did not have access from public transportation, and is in a historically exclusive neighborhood—home largely to wealthy white individuals. The board worried that the house would not be a comfortable space for their expanded constituencies. The historical society needed a long-range master plan that would help them move beyond the bounds of their historic house and have broader impact across the city.

We benchmarked a range of historical societies and historic houses doing unusual or unexpected work, including some examples within their region, as well as national examples, like Lincoln's Cottage (Washington, DC) and the Alice Paul Institute (Mount Laurel Township, NJ). We thought we had assembled a diverse list with multiple different kinds of organizations that were each successful in their own way. As it turned out, the planning team waved that work aside. When we dug deeper, we realized the organization already had a very clear idea of where they wanted to go and were not interested in adapting ways in which other organizations had been successful. It turned out our role as the consultant was to help them articulate their new vision and define the kinds of spaces and resources they would need to bring it to life. While a bit unusual, the approach was effective, and the organization continues to make strides toward achieving its own vision. If your own benchmarking work is received in similar fashion, your job is to dig deeper. What makes the benchmarks seem off? By reexamining the thinking that supported the selection of the benchmarks, you may realize that you had a fundamental misunderstanding of the kinds of changes or new directions your organization is ready to pursue. While it can be disappointing, taking the time to develop consensus and excitement around new directions is one of the best indicators that your implementation will be successful.

Now that you have a clearer understanding of museums and other organizations that are your peers, it is time to start thinking about your museum. Who are some of its most important constituents? Where might your museum's center of gravity fall on the guitar pick diagram we described in chapter 2? In the next chapter, we will focus on identifying and defining the specific constituencies that your museum serves and refining the museum's center of gravity. This information will become the foundation for the rest of the planning process.

RESOURCE 4.1: BENCHMARK INTERVIEW QUESTIONS

If you choose to conduct interviews with benchmark institutions, these questions provide a starting point. Customize the questions below to maximize the takeaways for your organization.

Collections

- How would you describe your collection? What are the standout artifacts?
- What role do long-term exhibits play?
- Is your collection mostly stored on-site or off-site?

Exhibits

- Do you have a temporary exhibit program? If so, what has been most and least successful?
- What role do long-term exhibits play?
- Are exhibits developed in-house, contracted, or borrowed from other museums?

Programs

- What exhibit and program ideas have been most and least successful?
- Are public programs concentrated at certain times of the year, or are they more spread out?
- What is your average attendance for public programs?
- Are larger or smaller programs most successful for you?
- What kinds of topics and audience groups do you design programs around?
- How do you promote programs?
- Are your programs paid? Free with membership? Free to all? What do you think of these different models?
- Is your museum pursuing online, virtual, or hybrid programs? If so, have they been successful? What is working well?
- What is a "lesson learned" about programming you would like to share?

Numbers

- Do you track visitation by age group or other categories? If so, what are the breakdowns?
- How many members do you have?
- Can you tell me more about specific costs for a program, including staff time, materials, speaker fees, etc.?
- Can you share some information about utility costs or green energy use?
- What are the typical costs to care for collections?

Staff

- What are the departments in your museum? How many staff in each?
- Has the number of staff increased or decreased in recent years? Specific to certain departments?
- Where would more staff be helpful?
- Is staff mostly full-time? Part-time? Volunteer?
- What skill sets are most useful in staff [conducting the activity you are interested in learning more about]?

Building/Facilities

- What spaces in your building get the most use?
- What spaces work the best?
- What advice would you give someone designing a new [facility or aspect of facility]?
- Is your facility climate-controlled to museum standards? If not, are there plans to address that?
- How is your facility addressing the challenges of climate change?
- What kinds of spaces are most useful to have adjacent to each other?
- How does on-site and off-site space work at your museum? What goes where?

NOTE

1. As you review other museums, beware of the "one-third model." Sometimes, museum people reference a rule of thumb that a museum's revenue is ideally about one-third earned, one-third donated, and one-third endowed. In reality, we've seldom found this to be true. Instead, operating funds sources vary by museum type. As we saw in chapter 2, Community Museums receive the majority of their revenue through memberships and donations; Destination Museums earn the majority of their revenue; and Curatorial Museums often rely entirely on income from an endowment or institutional support.

5

Identifying the Museum's Constituent Groups

In this chapter, we explore the ways a museum's planning team can begin to understand and identify the unique constituent groups their museum serves and how each museum can leverage its resources to best address each constituent group's unique interests and needs. We will consider ways to identify and prioritize a museum's primary constituent groups and how to understand the differing desires and motivations for the ways each group might engage with the museum. At the close of this chapter, we provide templates and tips for developing lists of constituent groups, possible interview questions, and tips for interviewing. As we saw in chapter 2, we can divide museums into the three broad categories: Destination, Community, and Curatorial. In this chapter, we will develop a deeper understanding of how museums engage and interact with the people who can be included in each of these three broad categories.

As we begin to focus on the people whom a museum does or could serve, it is important to refer to these groups of people as *constituents* rather than visitors, attendees, or audiences. While many museums focus on visitor counts and visitor services to assess their success, thinking of visitor groups as merely one type of constituent prompts an important shift in a museum's mindset. While "visitor" implies someone coming to the museum, some of the most important people whom a museum serves may seldom visit in person. Using the word *constituents* allows for a much broader and richer understanding of the range of individuals and groups that a museum can engage with. It also corresponds with how museums are increasingly seeking to engage with their communities and the field's growing understanding of what museums do and how they do it. It used to be that the collections were what really mattered. Now museums understand that what a museum does needs to be relevant to target constituent groups and their lives. It used to be that museums let the artifacts speak for themselves. Now museums understand that the stories matter as much as the artifacts. And it used to be that museums will tell you what you need to know. Now museums understand that they need to engage their constituents in a conversation.

DEFINING MUSEUM CONSTITUENTS

We recommend a two-pronged approach to defining a museum's constituents. The first prong is a brainstorming session with the planning team, and the second is interviewing museum staff, stakeholders, and members of potential constituent groups. Brainstorming with the planning team provides an initial baseline for identifying constituent groups and may widen the perspective of team members. It also establishes a constituent group list that the interview process can test against in the second prong of defining constituents. The following is a suggestion for how a brainstorming session might proceed with a planning team.

The brainstorming session usually works best as an in-person meeting. When setting a time for the brainstorming session, also ask each member to think about all the constituent groups that the museum does serve, could serve, or would like to serve in the future. Encourage each member to also reflect on the museum's current DEAI work as they think about constituents. Each team member should come ready to share a list of constituents, setting aside practical considerations for the time being. (See Resource 5.1 for a sample, which includes definitions of constituents.) At the beginning of the meeting, ask each member to share their list of constituents and continue to brainstorm as many different constituent groups that are connected to your museum as you can. At this point, also think about the groups you are not serving, particularly groups that have not visited your museum in the past, but might benefit from, or simply enjoy, the museum's programs. Finally, work together to sort these groups into the Destination, Community, or Curatorial categories. One simple visual way to do this is by writing each constituent group on a sticky note and then sorting the notes into the categories of museums; this works equally well with digital tools like jamboards.

Below are some sample constituent groups broken down by category to get started. Keep in mind that every museum is different, and these lists are starting places—add the constituent groups that are missing and take out those that you cannot effectively serve or that are not present at your organization.

Destination

- Tourists/visitors to the region
- Visiting friends and relatives
- Pilgrims or "bucket list" visitors (people who have a special connection to the museum's topic or location who may travel very long distances to experience the real thing)
- Visitors going to another destination, such as visiting a university or attending a conference, sporting match, or concert who might also visit the museum while in the area. For example, a museum located next to significant university might get many visitors who are primarily in the area to visit the university, but who also visit the museum as part of the trip to understand more about the community
- Constituents with a specific interest they will travel to support (for example, a museum with a notable garden or with a significant furniture collection might list garden enthusiasts or material culture collectors as destination constituents)

Community

- K–12 students
- Homeschooling families
- Teachers
- Regional residents
- College/university students and faculty
- Subject matter enthusiasts (such as collectors) seeking repeated engagement
- Other communities of interest/affinity connected to the museum's topic
- Other communities connected to the museum's location/region
- Volunteers
- Retired residents
- Garden lovers (a museum with a garden may attract local gardeners as visitors, volunteers, or both)

- Creatives, include artists, poets, writers, musicians, and others who find the museum sparks creativity or provides a creative outlet for performances, readings, or exhibitions
- Affiliated cultural groups
- "Owners of the story" (the people whose lives or actions developed the stories, things, and ideas presented in your museum or continue to enact those ideas. For example, owners of the story at a civil rights museum would include activists who participated in civil rights protests and actions during the 1960s, as well as activists working on civil rights causes today)

Curatorial

- Scholars and researchers
- Collectors
- Future generations (who will benefit from having the same opportunity to study, view, or experience the materials, buildings, or other items in the future)
- Aspiring museum professionals who are seeking to learn the trade/craft of working in a museum in any department, not just curatorial

Of course, constituents may enact several categories during a visit or may move into different categories of the duration of their relationship with the museum. And there may be similar groups across the three big categories. A common overlap is garden constituents. A notable garden may attract destination constituents seeking to see the well-known garden, *and* it may also have regional community constituents who return to the garden regularly for inspiration and even volunteer to support its care and maintenance. In these cases, it is appropriate to list garden lovers (or another group) as both a community and a destination visitor group because while similar, each group has distinct needs and kinds of interaction with the museum. Small Historic House Museums are similar. They may attract some destination visitors, and they also depend on the support of a vigorous group of community volunteers for daily operations. At this point in the process, it is most productive to keep the constituent group list long and open to different possibilities. As the plan develops focus, the constituent groups will be narrowed to match that focus.

Some constituent groups, especially those like government or partner organizations, defy easy classification. This kind of group might be categorized as "Other Stakeholders." This group includes state or local governments; a larger organization that has some, but not complete, control over your organization; or nearby museums or nonprofit organizations with very similar or complementary collections or missions. Examples of this include a museum owned by a college, but operated by a nonprofit; the relationship between the National Park Service and National Heritage Areas; or a museum and a nonprofit working in the same region that both seek to preserve historic structures. In these cases, the other organization influences but does not control the museum's operations or finances, so it still needs to be engaged, informed, and satisfied with your trajectory. It is important to note these relationships. Still, use this category as sparingly as possible, and only for groups that truly do not fit into the other categories.

This categorized list will become the foundation with which you will begin to fully understand your constituents. The next step is to conduct interviews with staff, board members, and other key stakeholders and constituents specific to your museum's circumstances.

CONSTITUENT INTERVIEWS

It is important to engage a wide variety of people initially through interviews and later as part of workshops to ensure that every voice is heard and every idea is considered. Identifying the right people to interview depends on the museum, its organization and administration, and the desired outcomes of your planning project. Note that a wide range of people should be consulted, including those who are both enthusiastic about potential change and those who are skeptical. Use the interview process to bring as many voices into the planning as possible. When your supporters and community members feel heard early in the process, it sets the stage for building consensus around the details of a final master plan. For this reason, you may wish to conduct interviews with individuals who expect to be consulted or need to feel that their opinions and experiences are valued, even if they may not add much to the process. By interviewing them, you will begin to develop buy-in for change.

The checklist at the end of this chapter (Resource 5.2) offers a starting point for selecting thirty-five or more people to interview through one-on-one or small-group interviews. Note that more interviews may be required depending on the size of the museum and the complexity of the project; thirty-five is usually a good starting point for most small to medium projects. Thirty-five may seem like a lot of people and a big investment of time. It is. And it is critical to understanding your constituents and provides the foundation for building consensus around the plan. Often, interviews upend the planning team's thinking about the museum, and many times the ideas that become critical parts of the plan are first articulated by an interviewee. When people feel heard and that they can contribute, they are more likely to make concessions and come together to support the plan through the drafting process and through implementation. An investment of time on the front end will pay dividends in the end.

In these interviews, ask the interviewee to describe themselves, what kinds of activities and experiences they currently engage with at the museum (or why they don't engage) or what they are seeking from the museum, and ways they think the museum can change. Ideally, conduct as many one-on-one interviews as possible. If logistics or other concerns dictate grouping interviewees together, avoid interviewing more than three people together and make sure group members already know one another and are comfortable speaking openly with the others. To maximize what you can learn from a group or one-one-one interview, assure people that the interviews are confidential. Usually, thirty to forty-five minutes is enough for a one-on-one interview. Group interviews require an hour. It's best to keep interviews conversational and to follow the thread of the interviewees' concerns and interests rather than proceeding through a list of questions. Tips for interviewing are included as Resource 5.3, and a list of sample questions is provided in Resource 5.4.

As the interview process unfolds, you may get the question, "Why not a focus group?" The answer is relatively simple: focus groups are well suited to assessing a particular product, need, or question. That is, they are effective at assessing the potential impact of a specific intervention. Good focus group questions include: What would be the most effective program for students in grades three through five visiting the museum? What are the key elements of an exhibit on butterflies? And so on. Focus groups are not well suited to the long-term planning process outlined here. Henry Ford neatly summed up the general public's limited ability to conceptualize the future and to think outside the box, by (purportedly) saying, "If I had asked people what they wanted, they would have said faster horses." In our experience, focus groups can also inhibit participants from sharing their aspirations for the museum or their "wild ideas" for fear that they will be shouted down or seem too unmoored from current realities. Instead, to think long-term, individual, open-ended interviews are most effective.

After each interview, note any constituent groups the interviewee described or is a part of and compare them to the list you developed with the planning team. Add any group that is missing; note groups that were mentioned that were already on the list with a tally mark or similar. As the process continues, you may notice that certain groups come up repeatedly, while some are never mentioned at all. At the conclusion of the interviews, the planning team should assess the constituent list as it stands now. This updated list starts to reveal the groups that are most important for the museum to serve—the groups that are, or will be, the museum's center of gravity. If no center of gravity is apparent, developing a stronger focus may need to become a more important outcome of the planning process before other work can begin. Refining that focus can become an important aspect of the plan you develop. Remember, serving everyone means you serve no one effectively and you are falling short of your potential to meet your mission.

NEXT STEPS

With a clear idea of your primary constituents, it is time to determine what each group's motivations and needs are and what it will take to serve them effectively. We will use what we have learned about the museum's constituents in the next chapter to develop a logic model that will help us to broadly understand each constituent group's needs, how the museum can best meet those needs with activities and experiences of various kinds, the operational and facility consequences of the activities and experiences, and the mission- and money-related outcomes for each group of constituents. Identifying and prioritizing the museum's constituents will become the foundation of the planning work that follows in the remainder of this book.

RESOURCE 5.1: BRAINSTORMING SESSION HOMEWORK TEMPLATE

During this session, we will be developing a list of all the constituencies our museum serves now or could serve in the future. A *constituent group* is a narrowly defined group of people with distinct interests and motivations driving their engagement with the museum. Examples include students in grades 3–5, visiting friends and relatives, tourists, collectors, amateur artists, garden lovers, and many others. When defining a group, try to be as specific as possible: instead of "youth," state "students in grades 8–10" or "families with children"; instead of "adults," use "artists" or "lifelong learners." Once we have developed a list of constituents, we will work as a group to place each specific constituent group into one of the three broad categories: Destination, Community, and Curatorial.

Destination constituents are looking for a unique and engaging experience. They typically come to visit a museum on an irregular basis, often only once. They typically come in small groups, which may include family members and, often, visiting friends and relatives.

Community constituents have a continuing relationship with the organization through a wide variety of activities and experiences, including membership, programming, events, online activities, and educational programs. For most museums, community constituents can be divided into two groups:

- Regional constituents, who live nearby and can frequently engage with the museum.
- Affinity constituents, with a special interest in the organization's exhibits, programs, collections, or expertise.

Curatorial constituents are typically most interested in a museum's collections and their preservation and growth. Curatorial constituents can be a museum's most passionate advocates and most significant donors.

Please come to the session with three to five suggestions of constituent groups in mind, as defined above.

RESOURCE 5.2: INTERVIEW CANDIDATE SELECTION CHECKLIST

Staff

- Director (1)
- Staff department heads or leaders who can speak to development, marketing, finance, collections, and public program/education (5)
- A staff group interview (1)

Board Members

- Board chair (1)
- Significant board members who are engaged with the project (3)
- Someone with a strong understanding of the organization's past, like a former board president or founding member (1-2)

Donors

- Significant past or potential future donors (2)

Partner Organizations

- Partner organizations (other nonprofits) (4)
- Education partners (schools) (2)

Community Members

- Representatives of particular constituencies (for example, scholars, material culture enthusiasts, collectors, etc.) (3)
- Local community members (4)
- Local leadership, like a mayor, city council members, etc. (1-2)

From any of the above groups:

- Someone who was an active participant in the last major change, building project, or campaign the organization undertook (1-2)
- Someone who is enthusiastic about potential changes or new projects (2)
- Skeptics or others who could derail the project if not brought on board (2)

RESOURCE 5.3: TIPS FOR SCHEDULING AND CONDUCTING INTERVIEWS

- Schedule board members and other significant stakeholders for individual interviews. Put together small-group interviews for staff members or people with less immediate connections to the museum.
- Send a note introducing the planning process to all individuals you plan to interview. The note should come from either the director, the board chair, or both.
- For online interviews, set aside a few blocks of time each day for interviews. If possible, allow interviewees to schedule themselves using an online sign-up platform to decrease the amount of time you spend scheduling.

- Offer in-person as well as virtual/telephone interviews to give interviewees flexibility.
- Develop an interview guide (see Resource 5.4) and send it to your interviewees in advance of the interview so they have a sense of the kind of information you are looking for.
- Approach the process as a listening exercise—this is not the time to try to sell interviewees on particular ideas. All the best ideas are likely already in the room—you just need to listen for them and use them to inform the plan.
- Ask open-ended questions.
- Ask clarifying or follow-up questions to make sure you understand each individual's point of view.
- Seek to understand what the interviewee sees as the museum's assets or successes as much as what they would like to see to change.
- Ask for help—to whom can the interviewee connect you who might be helpful?
- Make no promises about what might change; only confirm that the interviewee's feedback will be given consideration as the process continues.
- Respect the interviewee's time and start and end promptly.
- Take notes! Recording the interview may raise questions about confidentiality.
- Know when to stop. When you've interviewed a cross-section of individuals and you start hearing the same things, you've probably learned all that you can from the interview process.

RESOURCE 5.4: SAMPLE INTERVIEW DISCUSSION GUIDE

The following guide is offered as a starting point. The planning committee should weigh in on the specific questions to pose.

Background

[Museum Name] is starting the process of developing a long-range master plan to inform future development of the museum's activities, site, and facilities.

As a first step in our planning, we will meet with staff, board, and community members who can help us to understand the needs and opportunities that will inform potential changes to the site, buildings, and museum activities. During our meetings, we will ask you to share ideas and insights and to identify resources, constraints, opportunities, and challenges that are important for us to understand.

Issues for Discussion

The list below outlines some of the topics we are especially interested in hearing about. We know that not everyone will be able to respond to every issue, and we expect that many other ideas will come up as we learn more about the museum.

- What do you like best about the museum? How would you like to see it develop in the future?
- What are the museum's most pressing needs? What else needs to change or be updated?
- How can the museum better serve its visitors, supporters, and other important groups?
- Who is the museum for? Local community members? Tourists? School groups? Researchers? Subject matter aficionados? College students? Creatives? [Add local possibilities.]

- Which groups are most important? What kinds of exhibits, programs, and other experiences will best serve each group?
- How can the museum best interact with [significant stakeholder group]?
- What can we learn from other museums you know or may have visited?
- What are your wild ideas? What other opportunities, alternatives, and possibilities should be considered?

Please note: All discussions and comments are confidential. We will use the information we gather to make recommendations and build our reports, but nothing will be attributed to any individual or group.

About the Interviewers

[If they are not universally known to interviewees, provide the names of the people who will conduct the interviews here, along with brief bios (1 sentence or fewer).]
Anything else we should know? Email [NAME]: [email]

6

Developing the Constituent Logic Model

At this point, you've gathered a lot of data, you've talked to a lot of people, and you may feel like all the possibilities—ranging from the feasible to downright *out there*—have been presented to you. And, realistically, you probably *have* heard most of the possibilities. Now it's your job to pull all the ideas together and prioritize those that have merit into a preliminary plan for your museum. To do this initial analysis, we use a tool we call the Constituent Logic Mode. The Constituent Logic Model provides a framework to synthesize and organize all the information gathered during the background research, the interviews, and the benchmarking. It is the most important tool in your planning tool kit because it connects constituent interests and needs to the desirable outcomes for both the constituent and the museum. The logic model becomes the foundation of the museum's master plan.

WHAT IS A LOGIC MODEL?

What, exactly, is a logic model? The Community Tool Box at the Center for Community Health and Development at the University of Kansas defines a *logic model* as

> a picture of how your effort or initiative is supposed to work.... Effective logic models make an explicit, often visual, statement of the activities that will bring about change and the results you expect to see for the community and its people. A logic model keeps participants in the effort moving in the same direction by providing a common language and point of reference.[1]

Logic models are sometimes referred to as road maps, program frameworks, or theories of change. They can take a variety of forms, including bubble charts, maps/pathways, tables, or other visual representations that demonstrate the pathways and feedback loops that bring about the stated goal or fulfill the desired outcomes. Logic models can be built forward (starting with the goal or change) or backward (starting from the desired outcome). One effective way to think about the difference in these approaches is by connecting them to questions. When building a logic model "forward," the question to keep asking is, "But why?" That is, why are you doing it—what is the outcome you are pushing to achieve? When building backward, the question becomes, "But how?"[2] That is, we know the why or outcome, and now we need to spell out what we must do to get there. Either approach will get to the heart of a logic model's value, and often it is helpful to work both forward and backward.

Before we move further, it is worth noting that the word *logic*, has many definitions. For our planning process, *logic* refers to our capacity to make sense of complex phenomena by discovering patterns. That is, we use the logic model is to understand how things work—the logic—of the phenomena we want to affect.[3] The goal is to give the team a clear set of actions to take to achieve the desired outcomes. The logic model used in this planning process is a series of "If . . . then . . ." statements structured into a table with six columns. Each column builds on the information developed in the columns preceding it. That is, the logic of the table initially flows from left to right as follows: 1) Groups of users whom the museum does or could serve, 2) who are interested in or motivated by these specific types of things or activities, and 3) who would be engaged by specific kinds of activities and experiences, 4) which require specific types of staffing and operating support, 5) that need specific kinds of facilities, and 6) which will result in specific outcomes for each group. This flow is best illustrated with an example. Since logic models are inherently visual, please take a minute to review Template 6.1 before reading further. You can also see a completed logic model for a small literary museum in Resource 6.2.

Constituents that the museum serves	Who are interested in the following types of things	And would be engaged by these kinds of experiences	Which require staffing and operating support	And appropriate facilities	And result in the following outcomes:
Constituent Groups	**Interests, Needs, Motivations, and Desires**	**Activities and Programs**	**Staffing and Operational Needs**	**Facility Needs**	**Mission & Money**
DESTINATION					
COMMUNITY					
CURATORIAL					

Template 6.1 Logic Model Template

DEVELOPING YOUR LOGIC MODEL

Before you begin, keep in mind that developing a logic model is not easy! The first draft of the logic model is likely to be messy and inconsistent, with some cells too long, others too short, and several simply muddled or unclear. But the process of sorting and refining the information within the logic model, in discussion with other team members, plays an essential role in building understanding and consensus about the foundations of your master plan. When you are beginning to develop a logic model, it is often best to follow a three-step process. In the first step, one member of the planning team completes a preliminary rough draft. Then, they work with a teammate or two to discuss, reorder, and refine the table into a second draft. In the third step, the team presents their second draft to the rest of the planning committee for discussion and further refinement.

We work through developing an example logic model on the following pages. As we do so, you can follow the process of adding information to the model in Resource 6.1. In this example, we will limit the model to three constituent groups that are important for many museums. Your museum's logic model may contain these and will likely contain many more groups across all three categories.

- Visiting friends and relatives (Destination constituents)
- K–12 students (Community constituents)
- Scholars and researchers (Curatorial constituents)

Column 1: Constituents

We begin by populating the first column of the table with the constituents you outlined in chapter 5. Starting with the constituent groups listed under Destination, place one constituent group in each box in column one, adding more rows to the table as needed. Then do the same thing with Community constituents and Curatorial constituents. Note that the number of constituent groups in each category can vary substantially. That is okay—each museum will have a different balance of constituent groups. For quick reference, it may help to color-code the chart boxes to keep track of the major categories—we typically use green for Destination, blue for Community, and yellow for Curatorial. Other colors can work as well. With the constituent groups filled in, we can now begin to work across the logic model. In the sample, we will use the three groups listed above.

Column 2: Interests, Needs, Motivations, and Desires

In the second column, we begin to understand the constituents. What do they care about? Why might they want to visit? What must they accomplish or experience in order to feel like they had a fulfilling visit? (That is, do they want a social experience? An educational experience? Something else?) What are their unique needs? Here are some of the interests, needs, motivations, and desires for the example groups:

Visiting Friends and Relatives

- Something unique to do while visiting
- A social experience
- Multigenerational activities
- Learning about something unique to the region or town they are visiting

K–12 Students

- Out-of-class experiences that bring what they are learning to life or provide an opportunity to apply skills in new ways
- New or renewed interest in a particular subject
- Inspiring creative or career interests development
- Stronger connection to community (most often applicable to history or other museums that describe a community's experiences)
- Improved learning outcomes/success in the classroom

Scholars and Researchers

- Study of unique collections, including archives
- Opportunity to make new discoveries or draw new conclusions

Developing the Constituent Logic Model

Column 3: Activities and Experiences:

The third column is the place to describe the things the museum does or can do to meet the interests and needs outlined in column 2. These activities are all grouped as *Activities and Experiences*, an umbrella term for everything a museum does to serve the public—it often begins with collections and includes permanent and temporary exhibits, public programs, education programs, volunteer programs, outreach efforts, festivals or special events, and more. To identify these, begin by looking at the interests, needs, motivations, and desires you identified. What kinds of activities would best meet those? As you develop your list of activities and experiences, think about not only what your museum already does that serves a particular group, but also what you could do to broaden your reach. Be sure to include a mix of current and future or possible activities and experiences. We sometimes use regular text to indicate activities that are part of current operations and italicized text for potential new activities or experiences. This helps keep current operations clearly delineated from aspirations. This approach can be used in any of the columns where new opportunities are contemplated. Let's look at some activities and experiences that meet the needs of the sample groups.

Visiting Friends and Relatives

- Memorable long-term exhibits
- Orientation to the geographic area or topic
- Guided or self-guided experiences
- Hands-on experiences that draw multigenerational groups together
- Activities that promote memory-making/Instagrammable or sharable moments

K–12 Students

- Field trips
- Bringing the "real thing" to their classroom
- Immersive programs and/or creative use of technology
- After-school and summer programs
- Hands-on learning activities (from milking a cow to sailing a boat)
- Programs that invite students to bring their caregivers back to the museum
- Internship or volunteer opportunities

Scholars and Researchers

- Secure and accessible collections-storage areas
- Ability to access resources and collections in person and online
- Research-room hours that match their schedules
- Connection with staff who are knowledgeable about the collections the researcher is working with

Column 4: Operational Needs

The fourth column lists the staffing and other operational requirements needed to make happen the activities and experiences outlined in the previous column. This is not a place for a full staffing model, but it is a way to identify key personnel and other operational components that are needed to bring an activity to life. For example, a successful temporary exhibit needs curatorial staff to develop and mount it, program staff to offer events related to it, visitor-services staff to welcome people coming to see it, and depending on your museum, maybe security staff to help manage visitors and protect exhibits and/or marketing staff to promote it. Try to be realistic without getting into the weeds; "museum educators" is sufficient for an in-school program because you know you'll need more than one person to make it happen. Don't worry about listing numbers, whether the positions are part-time or full-time, or other specifics; these are placeholders to help others (board members, in particular) to understand that museum programs and activities do not occur in a fiscal vacuum and that additional staff resources may be needed to support exciting new programs. A full staffing model will be developed later in the process; note that the same staffing need can be identified in multiple rows if it also applies to the activity. Sample logic-model entries might include:

Visiting Friends and Relatives

- Visitor-services staff (admissions, museum store, and café)
- Point of Sale software for tickets, gift shop, etc.
- Program staff (may or may not be required, depending on the activities you've outlined)

K–12 Students

- Education director
- Museum educators
- Visitor-services staff

Scholars and Researchers

- Curator and/or archivist
- Registrar and/or collection manager
- Collections-management software
- Research librarian or collections assistant

Column Five: Facility Needs

The fifth column outlines the kinds of facilities or spaces within a facility needed to accommodate the people and activities you have described so far. Again, no need for a high level of detail. "Flexible classroom space" is enough; "two or three 500-square-foot classrooms that can accommodate clean and dirty activities" is too much at this stage. Be sure to include both front-of-house (public facing) and back-of-house spaces (collections processing and exhibit prep).

As you think about facilities, be sure to include outside needs, as well. If you hold outdoor events, how will people access those areas? If you are welcoming groups coming in buses, where can buses drop off participants? Park? Do you have enough parking for regular visitors, too? Sample logic-model entries might include:

Visiting Friends and Relatives

- Welcoming and accessible orientation area
- Introductory/long-term exhibit space
- Space for hands-on activities
- Easy navigation to the museum and parking
- Good wayfinding inside and outside the building
- Excellent museum shop

Developing the Constituent Logic Model

K–12 Students

- Multipurpose rooms or classrooms
- Bus dropoff
- Plentiful bathrooms near the entrance and classrooms
- Space to store coats, lunches, and belongings
- Space to eat lunch

Scholars and Researchers

- Comfortable, dedicated research areas with good lighting and plug-ins
- Appropriate collection- and archive-storage areas to insure long-term preservation

Column 6: Outcomes (Mission and Money)

The final column describes the outcomes for each specific constituent group—what will happen if you provide the activities and programs outlined, along with the support staff and facilities? Common mission outcomes include inspiring respect for or interest in a topic, preserving or telling specific stories, engaging the regional community, and more. Typical money outcomes include admission, membership, program fees, donations (both cash and items for the collection), museum store or café revenue, and government or foundation grants. Museum people often don't like to talk about money, but successful nonprofits must change lives *and* raise or earn the money to continue to provide inspiring activities. Here are some mission and money outcomes for our sample groups.

Visiting Friends and Relatives

- Connection to their local hosts; potential to develop ongoing relationships
- Positive word-of-mouth
- Admission fees
- Museum shop/café revenue

K–12 Students

- Reaching of new audiences, which may include underserved or untapped audiences
- Inspiration of the next generation
- Connection to students' caregivers (additional engagement and membership potential)
- Potential grant and philanthropic support

Scholars and Researchers

- Original research
- Exhibition resources
- Potential publicity and/or publications
- Legacy gifts and endowment support

RESOURCE 6.1: COMPLETED LOGIC MODEL AS DESCRIBED IN THIS CHAPTER. MUSEUM INSIGHTS

Constituents that the museum serves Who are interested in the following types of things And would be engaged by these kinds of experiences

Constituent Groups	Interests, Needs, Motivations, and Desires	Activities and programs
DESTINATION		
Visiting Friends and Relatives	• Something unique to do while visiting • A social experience • Multi-generational • Learn about something unique to the region or town they are visiting	• Memorable long-term exhibits • Orientation to the geographic area or topic • Guided or self-guided experiences • Hands-on experiences that draw multigenerational groups together • Activities that promote memory making/instagramable/sharable
COMMUNITY		
K-12 Students	• Out-of-class experiences that bring what they are learning to life or provides an opportunity to apply skills in new ways • New or renewed interest in a particular subject • Develop career interests • Stronger connection to community (most often applicable to history or other museums that describe a community's experiences) • Improved learning outcomes/success in the classroom	• Field trips • Bringing the "real thing" to their classroom • Immersive programs and/or creative use of technology • After school and summer programs • Hands on learning activities • Programs that invite students to bring their caregivers back to the museum • Internships or volunteer opportunities
CURATORIAL		
Scholars and Researchers	• Study unique collections, including archives • Opportunity to make new discoveries or draw new conclusions	• Secure and accessible collections storage areas • Ability to access resources and collections in person and online • Research room hours that match user's schedules • Connect with staff knowledgeable about the collections the researcher is working with

RESOURCE 6.1: (CONTINUED)

Which require staffing and operating support	And appropriate facilities	And result in the following outcomes:
Staffing and Operational Needs	**Facility Needs**	**Mission & Money**
• Visitor services staff (admissions, museum store, and café) • Point of Sale software for tickets, gift shop, etc. • Program staff	• Welcoming and accessible orientation area • Introductory/long-term exhibit space • Space for hands-on activities • Easy navigation to the museum and parking • Good wayfinding inside and outside the building • Excellent museum shop	• Connection to their local hosts; potential to develop ongoing relationship • Positive word-of-mouth • Admission fees • Museum shop/café revenue
• Education director or lead • Museum educators • Visitor services staff	• Multi-purpose rooms or classrooms • Bus drop-off • Plentiful bathrooms • Space to store coats, lunches, and belongings • Space to eat lunch	• Reach new audiences, which may include underserved or untapped audiences • Inspire the next generation • Connect to students' families (outreach and membership potential) • Potential grant and philanthropic support
• Curator and/or archivist • Registrar and/or collection manager • Collections management software • Research librarian or collections assistant	• Comfortable, dedicated research areas with good lighting and plug-ins • Appropriate collection and archive storage areas to insure long-term preservation	• Original research • Exhibition resources • Potential publicity and/or publications

PUTTING THE LOGIC MODEL TO USE

The completed logic model clearly demonstrates who your museum does or could serve and the kinds of activities programs and operating models serving them would require. Likely, the completed first-draft logic model will be pages long and seem daunting to review, let alone enact. So many possibilities! This is where the work gets interesting. Making decisions about which constituent groups to prioritize is where we begin to understand what a plan for the future will look like.

With all options and outcomes on the table, it is time to prioritize the museum's future constituents. This is where we can use the logic model to work backward, from the right side back to the left. By sorting the rows based on the strength of their mission and money outcomes, you can begin to see which groups are most important and most readily served. The two critical questions are: Whom do you most want to serve? Where is the money going to come from? The constituent groups with the clearest answers should move to the top of the chart, ignoring the broader groupings (Destination, Community, and Curatorial) for the time being.

Next, take a look at the list to reconsider groups whose mission and money outcomes are least compelling. Generally, these are groups whom the museum cannot effectively serve without significant changes to the mission, new facilities, or substantial new sources of funding. If serving them well requires significant additional staff or the construction of a major facility and the planning team does not see either option as feasible, it is not appropriate to prioritize these groups. On the other hand, if a major capital campaign is being contemplated, and the museum is willing to make the changes needed to facilities or operations to serve a new constituent group effectively, it is fine to move them up toward the top, even if current facilities and staffing do not meet their needs. Once all the groups have been discussed and prioritized, review the remaining groups. Should some be eliminated? Or could some be rolled up into one larger group that generally reflects their overlapping needs and interests? Some common examples of this are combining K–12 students, homeschool families, and teachers into one group; another is combining specific groups of residents into one group of regional residents.

As you begin to narrow down the constituents in the logic model, keep a close eye on two factors: mission and money outcomes, and the team's excitement about serving particular groups. Both factors are critical to the success of a master plan that meets the needs of the groups you have prioritized. Continue to eliminate groups and combine groups until you have a model that is simple and direct. Consider having three to four groups represent your primary focus, two to three for your secondary focus, and one to two for your tertiary focus, then work to limit the table to two pages. For example, if your museum is a Community Museum that leans toward Destination, you might have three constituent groups under Community, two under Destination, and one under Curatorial.

For existing museums, it can be helpful to go back to the guitar-pick diagram developed in chapter 2 and evaluate what changes you might see in that diagram based on the work the team has done with logic model. Does your center of gravity become more Community and less Curatorial? Do you see opportunities in becoming more of a Destination Museum? Do you need to double down on collections and minimize the distractions of school programs? In the end, flexibility is important. All these questions will continue to reverberate throughout the planning process. Property may become available, a significant donor may move out of state, or the city may decide it needs the museum's current building for another purpose. Understanding your core constituents will help to guide you through these challenges.

After defining your core constituents, it is time for another DEAI check-in. How are the priority groups reflective of your DEAI work? If they are reflected, then it is likely that the master plan you are developing will effectively weave into the museum's DEAI work and continue to advance DEAI as part of the museum's mission. If they are not reflected, it may be time for a second look at both the museum's DEAI work and its constituent priorities. What is out of alignment? How might both adjust to

RESOURCE 6.2: SAMPLE LOGIC MODEL FOR A HISTORIC HOUSE MUSEUM FOCUSING ON A LITERARY FIGURE. MUSEUM INSIGHTS

Sample of Summarized Logic Model

Constituents	Interests, Needs, Motivations, and Desires	Activities and Experiences
Destination • Cultural Tourists • Literary Pilgrims • Visitors to the region	• Learn about the poet and her poetry at her home	• Tours and Programs • Studio Sessions • Orientation film and exhibit • Interpreted landscape
College Community • College students, faculty, admin, and alumni	• A distinctive part of the College that provides unique learning and creative opportunities and internships	• Student-focused literary and arts programming • Formal internship program • Programs and events related to College events
Affinity Community • The poet's devotees • Poets and writers	• Engage directly with the poet at her home • Find inspiration and connection with others	• Social media outreach and communities • Temporary exhibits • Extended tour options
Regional Community • Arts and culture enthusiasts • K-12 Students • K-12 Teachers	• Literary programming • Students (and teachers) engaged with the poet's life and poetry	• On-site activities and programs • Funded field trips • Onsite teacher institutes and workshops
Curatorial/Generative • Scholars and researchers • Poets and writers	• Touch the poet's life • Connect with other contemporary scholars, poets, and writers at her home	• Collections • Readings and workshops • Recognition and awards • Places for independent writing or reflection

RESOURCE 6.2: (CONTINUED)

Operational Needs	Facility Needs	Outcomes
• Program staff • Visitor services staff • Self-guided options	• Welcoming and accessible orientation area • Authentic buildings and landscape • Contemplative space	• Admissions, program fees, and store revenue • Positive word-of-mouth • Donations & membership
• College outreach curator • Internship coordinator • Event staff	• Welcoming and accessible • Seminar rooms • Intern workspace • Flexible gathering space	• Support from alumni • Increased engagement between the museum and the college(s) • Internship candidates • Membership, donations, and advocacy
• Staff for extended guided tours • Drop-in programs • Exhibits curator • Social media management	• Welcoming and accessible orientation area and exhibit spaces • Places for contemplation • Distinctive museum shop	• Deeper engagement with the poet's life and poetry • Long-term connections with the museum
• Public program and exhibit staff • Education coordinator and part-time educators	• Orientation and exhibit areas • Bus drop-off & parking • Program and classroom spaces • Authentic buildings and landscape	• Community support • Engaged teachers • Inspired students • Positive word-of-mouth • Progress in reaching underserved audiences
• Chief Poetry Officer • Program Coodinator • Program Staff	• Space for readings, lectures, and workshops • Collection storage and support spaces • Space for independent writing, reflection, and research	• Inspired poets and writers • Increased scholarship • Continued philanthropic and granting support

Developing the Constituent Logic Model

reflect where the museum wants to be going and the most effective ways it can do DEAI work? These are very difficult questions. Still, grappling with them now will significantly improve both the planning process and the museum's commitment to DEAI in the years ahead. With the solid foundation of a detailed and flexible logic model, the museum can now begin development of a detailed master plan, which will include plans for the museum's activities and experiences, operations, and facility needs.

NOTES

1. Community Tool Box Team, "Chapter 2, Section 1. Developing a Logic Model or Theory of Change," University of Kansas Center for Community Health and Development, https://ctb.ku.edu/en/table-of-contents/overview/models-for-community-health-and-development/logic-model-development/main.
2. Ibid.
3. Ibid.

7

Activity and Experience Planning

Now that the Logic Model is complete, we shift our focus from constituents to activities and experiences. Where the Logic Model is organized by constituent groups, the Activity and Experience Plan uses the information in the Activity and Experience column of the Logic Model to identify ways in which the museum can serve multiple groups with the same activities. Typically, the more constituent groups an activity serves, the more effective that activity will be in helping to fulfill the museum's mission. The plan developed in this chapter becomes the basis for developing accurate staffing, operational, and facility needs in the next stages of the planning process.

A typical Activity and Experience Plan is a narrative outline of the ways in which your museum will serve your constituents. The plan usually has six to twelve entries. It is important to remember that the Activities and Experiences Plan describes, in outline form, *all* the things your museum does to meet the interests, needs, and desires of the constituent groups you identified, outlined, and prioritized in the logic model. In the first draft of this plan, be sure to include activities and experiences that you both offer now, and could offer in the future. Being expansive at this point will give you flexibility if funding, site, zoning, or other constraints prevent you from doing all the things your desired constituents might find meaningful.

The activity and experience categories outlined below are a starting place for developing an Activity and Experience Plan. The categories group similar activities together and begin to structure the plan. Keep in mind that few museums will have all these categories, and most will need to add or alter these categories to reflect their unique operations. If our thirty years of museum planning has taught us one thing, it is that there is no one-size-fits-all museum!

- Visitor Reception and Orientation
- Long-Term Exhibits
- Temporary or Traveling Exhibits
- Tour or Docent-led Experiences
- Engagement with Partners or Parent Organizations
- Public Programs
- Programs for Teachers
- Programs for School Groups
- Programs for Youth and Families
- Out-of-School Programs
- Community-Building Events
- Internships, Fellowships, and Apprenticeships

- Citizen Science Programs
- Volunteers
- Online Happenings/Virtual Engagement
- Research and Publications
- Collections and Curation
- And any others suited to your museum's unique circumstances

Each museum will need to select the categories that fit its mission. Some museums might use many of the categories, while another's mission might mean they use only a few. Below are two examples of the categories picked by two different kinds of museums.

An Activity and Experience Plan for a history museum might include the following categories:

- Visitor reception
- Long-term exhibits
- Temporary exhibits
- Public programs
- Community-building events
- Programs for school groups
- Out-of-school programs
- Internships, fellowships, and apprenticeships
- Online happenings
- Research opportunities
- Collections storage and curation

An Activity and Experience Plan for a museum with an outdoor education focus might use these categories:

- Site orientation
- Gateway activities
- Outreach programs
- Science and stewardship programming
- Outdoor programming
- Administrative functions

BUILDING AN ACTIVITY AND EXPERIENCE PLAN

In the sections below, we dive into these categories and provide examples of the kinds of activities and experiences that might fit into each one. Following the description, we will discuss the impact on constituents, operations, and facilities, denoted by italic text.

Visitor Reception and Orientation

This category describes how you welcome visitors to your museum, how you orient them and provide information, including about any other amenities you are offering. Reception and Orientation includes both personnel services (a staffed welcome desk or similar) and site interventions, like wayfinding along roads leading to your museum and on site, interpretation on your grounds or landscapes, and other signage. Orientation may also include activities like showing a film or presenting a short exhibit designed to give all visitors the same foundation for their visit.

This section also includes amenities, like a museum shop or café. For some museums, amenities might also include wheelchair checkout and/or the storage of coats, larger bags, or any of the paraphernalia that comes with a visiting family. A military museum that serves veterans might prioritize having multiple wheelchairs available; a museum that is near a transportation center and serves many tourists might prioritize being able to store larger items for visitors; and yet another museum in a rainy climate might choose to have permanent racks for visitors to leave wet jackets and umbrellas.

- Usually, activities in this category serve many of the *constituent groups* you have identified because they mark the beginning of a visitor's experience at the museum, whether coming for an exhibit, a program, or a special presentation.
- Typical *operating considerations* include open hours aligned with visitor needs, needed numbers of visitor-services staff, and staffing supporting amenities like the museum shop or café.
- *Facility requirements* will vary depending on the activities, but they must always include ready access to restrooms. Once "rested," most visitors then need a dedicated space for reception and orientation, including a welcome desk of some variety and space for visitors to orient themselves before engaging with visitor-services representatives. The size of the reception desk will depend on the space and how many visitors typically come to the museum. Other activities, like watching a film or observing an orientation exhibit will also require specialized, dedicated spaces. As important as the greeting space are the back-of-house areas needed to support visitor services and the operation of the museum store and café.

Long-Term Exhibits

Long-Term Exhibits include exhibit experiences that are integral to the museum and that are expected to remain on view for ten to fifteen years. (Note that we prefer the term *long-term exhibits* to *permanent exhibits*, because it reflects the reality that exhibits benefit from periodic refreshes that consider new knowledge, new technologies, and changes in museum operations over time.) Generally, long-term exhibits showcase each museum's core collections and stories and take forms appropriate to the museum's primary constituents, subjects, and mission.

- Long-term exhibits will serve many, but not all, of the *constituents* you have identified. For regular visitors, the long-term exhibits are a backbone and may include "eternal verity" objects or experiences that are part of every visit. For new visitors, long-term exhibits provide background and context for the museum's other exhibits and experiences.
- *Operating considerations* for long-term exhibits may include gallery staff or security staff, as well as curatorial staff to develop and maintain the exhibit.
- *Facility requirements* for long-term exhibits depend entirely on what is being exhibited; they may include functional adjacencies, temperature, humidity, lighting, and other standards for preservation set by your museum's curator.

Temporary or Traveling Exhibits

Temporary or Traveling Exhibits are a chance to showcase different objects and stories and give regular visitors a reason to return. Temporary exhibits typically include traveling shows developed by other museums, in-house exhibits, crowd-sourced exhibits, or exhibits featuring contemporary creators in your museum's region.

- Temporary exhibits best serve *constituents* in the Community category, although they will also serve Destination visitors who are coming to the museum as a onetime visitor.
- *Operational considerations* can include exhibit rental costs, handling and mounting, security, publicity, etc. Temporary exhibits also require a strong curatorial team to develop and mount exhibits, as well as gallery/security staff as needed, and they typically benefit from program staff, who can develop programming around the exhibit to make the most of the effort to host it or produce it.
- A museum's *facilities* may constrain the kinds of temporary exhibits your museum can mount. Traveling exhibits have minimum-space requirements and may require security or specific HVAC controls. Even exhibits developed in-house will have to work within the space available.

Tour or Docent-Led Experiences

Tours include both guided and self-guided experiences. Guided tours are led by a staff member or volunteer and offer visitors an interpreted visit to an exhibit, a gallery, or a structure like a historic house. Walking tours are a type of guided tour that takes visitors outside into landscapes and communities. Self-guided experiences are visitor-directed and may take all the forms of guided tours. Self-guided tours may use media like audio guides, an app on a smartphone or tablet, or a paper guide that allows visitors to access content at their own pace. Self-guided walking tours, landscape tours, or historic trails often combine a paper or digital guides with interpretive signage located at various points on a tour route.

- Tour experiences most often serve *Destination constituents*, although, if tours change regularly, they may also appeal to some *Community constituent* groups.
- Tours are *operationally* staff-intensive—even self-guided tours require some orientation. If media are provided, staff will have to charge and maintain the tablets, audio guides, or similar devices. When considering staffing requirements, it should also be kept in mind that in addition to staff to present programs, staff time will also be required to develop programs, train others in presenting them, and evaluate guides and the tour program once it is implemented to make sure it is successful.
- *Facility needs* include specific places for tours to gather and depart, a space for visitors to store coats or larger bags if these are not permitted on the tour, and, if in use, space for storing, charging, and maintaining audio guides, tablets, and the like.

Engagement with Partners or Parent Organizations

Depending on your museum's organizational structure, it may be important for you to engage with or support the activities of your partners or parent organizations. For example, if your museum is part of a university, you may be called upon to support events on campus or student activities. Or, if your museum has a close partnership with a similar museum or collecting institution, close cooperation will help both organizations meet their goals. For example, if your museum is the historic house where a notable author lived and wrote, the institution that holds the author's papers and manuscripts will be a key partner.

- Maintaining strong relationships with partners and parent organizations will allow you to more effectively serve the *constituent groups* that you share, typically Community or Curatorial.
- Managing partner relationships requires an investment in *staff time*. Relationships require people from both sides of the partnership to put in the work.
- While relationships don't necessarily need *facilities* to flourish, partners may provide facilities to each other that further each organization's goals. For example, a university partner may be able

to offer better long-term collection storage than a small historic house; meanwhile, the historic house can offer the university the chance to exhibit items in its collection without the challenges of running a museum. Other partners may offer your organization access to space you need occasionally—like an auditorium—but don't have at your museum.

Public Programs

Public Programs cover a wide swath of museum activities. They include things like lectures, talks, workshops, classes, and more, that are connected to the museum's content and mission.

- Generally, public programs serve adult audiences and meet the needs of *Community constituents*, though some Destination visitors may happily join in if their visit coincides with a program of interest.
- Public programs are *staff-intensive*. They require staff to design, promote, and present the program; depending on the size of a program, additional staff from visitor services or other departments may also be necessary to manage the program.
- Public programs may also have impacts on operations. For example, an evening program that takes place after the museum would normally be closed or extending daytime hours to accommodate a special event will change *staff* and other *operational requirements*. *Facility needs* vary greatly depending on the type of public program, and they may require classroom, workshop, or auditorium space, depending on the nature of the program. Depending on type, programs may also require space for material storage and preparation. Noting these needs here is especially important because programs are much less successful when they lack the facility support required.

Programs for Teachers

Programs for Teachers are intended to support teachers' professional development and encourage them to take advantage of the museum's education offerings in their own classrooms. Professional-development opportunities include teacher seminars, such as those sponsored by the National Endowment for the Humanities (NEH); employment opportunities, in which a teacher works as a guide or in the education department during the summer, then brings back materials to their classroom or school; or conferences in partnership with other organizations.

- Activities that engage *teachers* by going to schools or inviting them to the museum are intended to showcase what the museum has to offer and make it easier for teachers to set up a classroom visit, check out a traveling trunk, or book a field trip.
- Like public programs, teacher programs require an investment by the *staff*. The most successful teacher programs are supported by a dedicated education department or staff who can develop and present these programs.
- *Facility requirements* are often minimal for teacher programs—existing space for programs can be used, or if a teacher seminar is being hosted, space may be borrowed from other nearby organizations that have the kinds of space you need. Unsurprisingly, these programs serve teachers, and by extension, students. If neither is a priority constituent group, it's likely not worth investing in this type of specialized programming.

Programs for School Groups

Programs for School Groups can take a variety of forms, including visits to classrooms, traveling trunks, field trips, and virtual visits. A museum may offer school programs that serve specific age groups, or it may serve the whole K–12 spectrum, depending on staffing and the museum's themes.

- These programs serve *students and teachers*, as well as *homeschool families*.
- Like teacher programs, school programs require a dedicated and robust education department supported by *museum educators* to develop programming, manage scheduling, and bring programs to life, regardless of whether the visit is virtual, in-person at the museum, or in the students' classroom.
- School groups also have significant *facility requirements*, including bus drop-off and parking space, storage space for students' belongings, a space to eat lunch, and classrooms. Even virtual visits will require a dedicated space with effective camera and sound equipment (as well as a strong internet connection!) to be successful.

Programs for Youth and Families

Programs for Youth and Families are intended to bring young people and their caregivers to the museum. Programs may be structured, like workshops and tours, or unstructured, like craft stations and take-and-make activities.

- Youth and family programs typically serve *Community constituents* and can be a good way to bring new or underserved groups into your museum.
- Successful programs for these groups require an investment from the *education department staff* and, if trying to reach new groups, the work of an *outreach coordinator* or another ambassador from the target group working at your museum.
- *Facility needs* will vary depending on the program, but classroom space and ample parking will go a long way toward meeting most of these goals.

Out-of-School Programs

Out-of-School Programs include after-school, weekend, and summer programs designed to engage young people in learning and the museum's themes.

- Like programs for youth and families, these programs primarily serve *Community constituents*. In contrast to Programs for Youth and Families, however, out-of-school programs do not include caregivers or expect them to participate.
- Like other programs serving students, these programs require significant *staff time*.
- They also have similar *facility requirements* to Programs for School Groups. Summer programs may also have outdoor space requirements.

Community-Building Events

Community-Building Events include festivals, community gatherings, and other events designed to bring together people from the same regional community or a community of interest. Examples might include a book festival at an author's home that brings together fans, the author, and writers more generally; an annual community winter craft fair hosted by a museum; and so on.

- These events usually serve *Community constituents* (though they can become a Destination event that attracts a wider range of participants), and they are at their best when they respond to the specific needs or desires from these constituents.
- This is important because this type of event requires an investment of *staff time* to plan, and it often requires all hands on deck (as well as the help of volunteers) to successfully execute.

- Because these are often larger events, they may be located off-site, or on-site in a large tent or temporary structure. They may or may not make use of the museum's existing *facilities*, though they are usually most successful when they retain close proximity to the museum.

Internships, Fellowships, and Apprenticeships

Internships, Fellowships, Apprenticeships, and similar opportunities provide critical experiences for young people thinking about a career in museums or people making a career shift to the museum field. These positions may be hosted by any of the museum's departments and should reflect the interests of the intern or fellow.

- Typically, interns and fellows are representatives of the *Curatorial* and *Community constituencies*.
- Interns and fellows require very little from a museum *facility* that is not already there.
- They do, however, require a consistent investment of *time and support from museum staff* in the department to which they are assigned so they can get the most out of their experience. Supporting interns and fellows can provide a pipeline for well-qualified candidates to enter the museum field, as well as support efforts to increase diversity within the field.

Citizen Science Programs

Citizen Science Programs include water-quality measuring, bird counts, native plant monitoring, and similar programs often linked to long-term museum-sponsored research projects.

- Citizen Science Programs provide *regular citizens* and *amateur scientists* the chance to collect data to support scientific inquiry.
- These programs usually require a substantial amount of involvement from *trained staff members* or partnering with *scientists and universities* with the equipment and know-how.
- Because these programs can require specialized equipment to conduct sampling or surveys and may require refrigeration or special processing, it is critical that your museum has the *appropriate facilities* to maintain equipment, store samples, and conduct analysis. Partnering with another organization may alleviate some of these needs; still, reflect carefully on your facility's capacity before beginning this type of program.

Volunteers

Volunteers provide support for many aspects of a museum's operations, especially public programs, visitor services, and education programs. As such, considering the volunteer program as a separate museum program may help direct dedicated resources to its support. While it may be tempting to think of volunteers only as retirees or caregivers not in the workforce, the most successful volunteer programs provide a range of positions, time commitments, and work hours that can align with a variety of work schedules and other life commitments, so that anyone with interest and skills that can benefit the museum can be invited to contribute.

- Volunteer programs typically serve *Community constituencies*, as the volunteers will come from your community. Even if the work of volunteers supports other groups, it is still very important to recognize that volunteers come from your community and are a Community constituent group.
- While volunteers may provide free labor, the recruitment, training, and retaining of skilled volunteers requires consistent and significant investment from the *museum's staff*.

- Volunteer *facility needs* differ little from those of staff, but keep in mind that volunteers need a place to store their belongings while volunteering, access to a break area, and, depending on the role, computer access or desk space. Designing extra capacity into back-of-house areas will help accommodate volunteers and make them feel welcome.

Online Happenings/Virtual Engagement

Online Happenings and Virtual Engagement include a wide range of programs that take place on the internet. Activities include active social-media pages (a given for museums today), online book clubs or discussion groups, virtual programs, hybrid programs (where an in-person/on-site program is streamed live to people online; virtual attendees may or may not be able to fully participate), or other events.

- Virtual programs most often serve a mix of *Community constituents*, both affinity and regional, who are interested in engaging more with the museum, and *Destination constituents*, who would like to be more engaged with the museum but cannot because they live too far away for it to be practical. The COVID-19 pandemic demonstrated that virtual programs can be very effective for certain groups. For example, the Emily Dickinson Museum discovered that many of their virtual programs had a worldwide reach, as Dickinson fans discovered new ways to engage with the life and work of the beloved poet. While surveys indicate that most museums have returned to a focus on in-person programs, virtual programs can still play an important role.[1] By evaluating the needs of your priority constituents, you will be able to determine what the appropriate emphasis is for this type of programming.
- Keep in mind that high-quality virtual programming requires both *facilities* and *staff* that can support it, including program spaces that are set up to accommodate hybrid programs, and dedicated recording spaces with good sound and lighting for fully virtual programs. Likewise, having IT and production support staff, whether contract or staff members, will ensure good quality and less stress for the staff presenting the program.

Research and Publications

Research and Publications includes access to the museum and its collections by scholars or other researchers that leads to publications, documentary films, exhibits, or similar results, as well as publications researched and produced by curatorial and other staff.

- Scholarly research typically reaches *Curatorial audiences*, while staff publications may reach a mix of Community and Curatorial audiences, depending on topic and level of detail.
- Supporting research and publication requires *staffing* to manage collections and *facilities* for both storing collections and providing access to researchers. The type of *needed facilities* will depend greatly on the type of collections and the number of researchers you anticipate accommodating.
- Researchers also require *staff time* to help researchers find the material they are seeking and supervising them while they are using it. Even staff-led research is time-consuming and may take staff away from other duties.

Collections and Curation

Collections and Curation describe the activities your museum engages in to develop and steward your collection, as defined by your collection management plan.

- These activities serve and are served by *museum staff* and formal amateur *Curatorial constituents*.
- Collections typically have very specific *facility needs*, including appropriate, secure storage; processing areas; and research areas. As collections grow over time, planning for the future growth of collections is critical.

Please note that these outlined activities are only a starting place. The most interesting and engaging parts of your museum may be something completely different. In fact, finding those unique differentiators, whether in terms of programs, constituents, or collections. can give your museum a strong foundation for future growth and development.

CRAFTING THE PLAN

After defining the categories of activities and experiences at your museum, you can now start to draft the Activity and Experience Plan. The resources section at the end of the chapter includes a template (Template 7.1) and some excerpts from sample plans (Resources 7.1 and 7.2), which may be helpful to review before starting. In developing your plan, each of your museum's categories will begin with a general overview of the activities and experiences to be included, then followed with constituents who will be served, operational considerations, and facility needs.

Begin by developing your own list of activities that fit within each category. Then, for each activity or experience, provide a few sentences on each of the following topics:

- Description of the program, activity, or experience.
- Constituent group(s) served. Note: Many of the activities will serve multiple constituent groups. The more, the better! Programs that serve multiple groups have greater impact across the museum.
- Operating considerations, including things like staffing, A/V support, maintenance, etc.
- Facility requirements, including things like parking, classrooms, restrooms, climate-controlled exhibit space, collections storage, exhibit prep areas, and back-of-house spaces.

Like you did in the logic model, keep operational and facility requirements simple in the Activity and Experience Plan; we will build out the details and analyze potential challenges in chapters 8 and 9. Likewise, do not leave out a potential program because your museum does not currently have the staffing or facilities to make it happen. This plan is aspirational. If the program has merit, keep it in the plan for now and assess it later in the next stages of the planning process. As much as possible, draw from what you have developed in the logic model and use this exercise to begin to flesh out the details of the activities and experiences your museum will offer. Once you have developed your Activity and Experience Plan, it will become a key reference point for the assessment of current operating models, facilities, and budgets, and the foundation for creating new models, changing facilities, and making any other adjustments you want to make in service of the long-range plan.

Now is another good time for a DEAI check-in. As you review the Activity and Experience Plan, ask yourself: Does it align with your DEAI work, especially as it relates to accessibility and inclusion? Because activities and experiences are some of the most public-facing parts of the museum, aligning them with the museum's DEAI work is one of the more powerful statements the museum can make about the sincerity of its work. Making a few adjustments here to better incorporate DEAI work, if necessary, will ensure that the master plan is in harmony with other museum efforts and make it more likely to succeed.

Of course, no activity or experience is successful without "back-of-house" support. The staff, equipment, and services needed to support the public-facing activities and experiences described above are as important to the museum's success as its exhibits, programs, and collections. Ways to estimate these requirements, which will vary substantially based on the staffing and spaces needed to support each museum's activities and experiences, will be outlined in the next chapters.

RESOURCE 7.1: EXCERPT OF AN ACTIVITY AND EXPERIENCE PLAN FOR AN HISTORIC HOUSE MUSEUM

Excerpts from an Activity and Experience Plan developed for an historic house museum that is located in a college town.

TEMPORARY EXHIBITS

Regular visitors to the museum will enjoy a wide range of temporary exhibits. Changing two to four times per year, these exhibits may feature items in the collection not usually on display, or the work of contemporary artists, writers, or poets within the community. Other temporary exhibits may be crowdsourced, or professionally produced exhibits will focus on a particular aspect of the museum's story that is lesser known, recently understood, or known to be of particular interest to visitors. Temporary exhibits may also be available online.

Groups Served

The museum's temporary exhibits will primarily serve the museum's Community constituents, including:

- Cultural tourists
- Literary pilgrims
- History enthusiasts
- Material culture enthusiasts
- Prospective students and families
- Visiting friends and relatives
- Arts and culture enthusiasts
- K–12 students
- Local college students and faculty
- School groups and Destination visitors, who may also enjoy the temporary exhibits

Operating Considerations

- Regular hours
- Visitor-services staff
- Exhibit-development team, including both curatorial and program staff

Facility Requirements

- Flexible space that can accommodate a variety of installation types of approximately 300 to 1,000 square feet
- Associated space for preparing exhibits
- Appropriate temperature controls and security for items displayed

Tour Experiences

The Museum will maintain a robust menu of personal, place-based experiences that matches the needs and expectations of a variety of visitors.

House Tours

Tours of the restored and furnished houses will remain the staple of the visitor experience, with enhancements as recommended by the Comprehensive Interpretive Plan currently under development.

Self-Guided Experience

The museum will open portions of both furnished houses for a self-guided experience. This experience will include both personnel services and digital interpretation that will give the participants multiple options for engaging with the space.

Self-Guided Tour of [Museum's town]

The museum will develop a self-guided tour of [town] that will be available digitally or in print. Stops should include places connected to the family's life in [town] and key events of the nineteenth and twentieth centuries that shaped their lives.

Landscape Tour (self-guided)

The museum may expand its current self-guided audio tour of the landscape, including considering additional interventions in the landscape such as GPS-triggered audio experiences.

Landscape and Conservatory Tour (guided)

The museum might develop a guided exploration of the landscape that includes discussion and demonstration of nineteenth-century gardening practices and tools and exploration of the conservatory, including its design and reconstruction process.

Groups Served

These tour programs will primarily serve the Destination group and will also appeal to some Community members:

- Cultural tourists
- Literary pilgrims
- Prospective students and families
- History enthusiasts
- Visiting friends and relatives
- Arts and culture enthusiasts
- Underserved audiences
- Homeschoolers
- Garden lovers
- Road Scholars
- Bus tour participants

- K–12 students
- Local college students and faculty

Operating Considerations

- Additional tour and interpretive options will not be possible without additional front-line and management staff who are trained in the offerings and new interpretive techniques
- Guide and visitor-services staff
- Regular hours; some seasonal offerings

Facility Requirements

- Gathering space (indoor and outdoor)
- Space for visitors to store excess belongings
- Long-duration parking

RESOURCE 7.2: EXCERPT OF AN ACTIVITY AND EXPERIENCE PLAN FOR A MID-SIZED MUSEUM IN A COMMUNITY WITH A LARGE SUMMER POPULATION

PUBLIC PROGRAMS

Seasonality

Public programs are designed for the museum's active season, May through October, and to its recovery season, November through April.

- Active Season programs provide a wide range of offerings serving island residents and visitors.
- Recovery Season focuses on serving the community of year-round residents, with a special focus on students.

ACTIVE SEASON PROGRAMS

The Weekly Happening

A regular early evening event could draw people to the museum's grounds. While the museum will be open, the primary goal is to introduce people to the location, not necessarily a deep dive into its exhibits. The event should be offered every week, so summer and part-year residents know they can count on it. Possibilities include a weekly cornhole tournament, an outdoor trivia night, a popular food truck or chef, or a mix of activities to draw people to the site.

Exhibit Programs

Each temporary exhibit will have a slate of related programming, including curator talks, lectures from scholars or experts, behind-the-scenes experiences, craft programs, and other offerings that engage visitors more deeply with the content and create positive buzz. Each temporary exhibit will also include a "recommended read" (for sale in the museum store) that will offer additional engagement with the topic. A discussion group for the book will meet toward the end of the exhibit's time. As opportunities arise, staff will also program around content within the permanent exhibits.

Museum Story Time

Invite each of the public libraries to bring their story time to the museum once or twice during the summer. Or, host a story-time event weekly at the museum, including a simple craft.

Grandparent Days

Days spread throughout the summer when grandparents in particular are invited to bring their grandchildren to the museum. Education staff will provide additional offerings, including special games and crafts.

Courses

If staffing is available, the museum can offer a range of short, summer courses targeted to summer and part-year residents. Course topics include history of the community, deep dives into specialized topics, learn-how classes for genealogy and historical research, and other classes, including plein-air painting and yoga. All will continue to draw groups back to the museum over the course of the summer.

Partnership/Hosted Programs

The museum will work with community partners, especially cultural organizations, to use the museum as a location for events, performances, and other activities.

Book Club

The monthly book club reads a book by a local author or a book about the region (fiction and nonfiction welcome) and discusses monthly at the museum.

RECOVERY SEASON PROGRAMS

During the winter season (November–April) public programs will bring a wide range of year-round residents to the museum at a time when many places are closed and the population is diminished. Programming focuses on community-building.

Weekly Lunches

The museum will expand on the soup-and-sandwich program previously offered and current brown-bag lunch program to give people a way to socialize with low cost. Consider partnering with organizations addressing food insecurity to help subsidize the lunch and encourage donations.

Evening Meetups

Open the museum space one evening a week for a BYOB gathering with no cost barriers, and provide simple games. Encourage people to bring their favorite games or projects to make the museum an informal gathering space in the winter for those who might want a little human contact but might not have much cash.

Hobby Historians

Open to all who love investigating community history, this group meets to discuss research projects, topics for investigation, and more. Each year, the best projects are published by the museum, and the authors are invited to present their work at a public symposium.

Community Curation

The museum will invite proposals from interested groups for developing a temporary exhibit that will be on view in a community gallery. The selected group(s) will work throughout the winter with curatorial staff to develop and mount the exhibition.

Weekend Family Programming

The museum will offer family programming during the winter geared to grades 3 to 8 with the goal of making the museum a fun family destination when much of the town closes for the winter.

Let's Talk about It

The museum will pick a theme for each winter (work, housing, schools, etc.) and explore how the community has experienced it in the past and also host discussion around the topic in the present. For example, if the topic of housing was selected, the museum might open the series with a session on the historical background of who lived in what kind of housing within the community. The next event might be a panel of local experts like builders and Realtors, and then close with a facilitated community discussion around the future of housing in the community.

Community-Building Events

The museum will host community-building events that celebrate the spirit of the community, past and present.

Community Outreach

The museum will participate in other events and happenings, such as the farmers market, agricultural fair, and others to share information about the museum and demonstrate to residents and visitors alike that the museum engages with the community inside other community spaces.

Community Fun

During the summer season, the museum hosts two or three fun community events that reinvigorate old traditions, like the full-moon party, or others, like beach bonfires, that are promoted as "old-fashioned fun." The events should be simple to present (staff time being the primary cost), free to low cost to attend, BYOB, and relatively unstructured: "Come hang out; we've got fire and a food truck"; "make your own fun" with simple things.

The Fall Cultural Festival

Led by the museum, this festival brings together visual artists, performing artists, makers, writers, and others from the community in a celebration of what they have created over the summer. The festival offers a taste of the remarkable cultural diversity and talent within the community and will be free or low cost to attend.

Summer Gala

The museum will continue its successful annual gala, which draws together the summer community around stories both familiar and unexpected.

Groups Served

Community events will primarily serve Regional Community constituents, including:

- Summer residents
- Philanthropists
- Program and nonprofit partners

Operational Considerations

- Event director
- Program director
- Program and event staff

Facility Requirements

- Flexible indoor and outdoor spaces that can accommodate a wide range of programs, performances, and presentations
- Provision for temporary restroom facilities for large-scale events
- Expanded parking

TEMPLATE 7.1: ACTIVITY AND EXPERIENCE PLAN TEMPLATE

Category 1 Title

Brief introduction describing the category.

List of Activities

In this section, list each of your planned activities with a brief description. Note any programs you currently offer with an asterisk, italics, or other notation.

List of Constituent Groups Served

Using the constituent groups listed in the Logic Model, list the groups that are served by these activities. Note that for some categories, like visitor orientation, the activities will serve nearly all the groups you identified.

Operating Considerations

Describes what kinds of hours, staff, and other operating considerations are required to make these programs happen.

Facility Requirements

Describes the preliminary requirements for the facility and the spaces within it to successfully host the activities described.

NOTE

1. Cuseum, *2022 Report: The State of Virtual and Hybrid Offerings at Cultural Organizations* (Boston: *Cuseum*, 2022), 4–6.

8

Staffing and Operational Needs

The staff, equipment, services, and other costs that are needed to support the public-facing activities and experiences of the museum are as important to the museum's success as its exhibits, programs, and collections. Spending the time getting staffing and operating costs right is not as exciting as developing exhibits and programs, but it is as important. Our goal in this chapter is to develop an operating plan and budget that outlines growth and changes to staffing and operations based on the ambitions of the Activity and Experience Plan. For an existing museum, this plan will update current operations. For a new museum, this planning provides a target for operations in the first few years after opening. It is essential to understand that this operating budget is a planning tool, not an operational guide. Our goal in the next few chapters is to find a balance between the size of the museum's building(s), its organization of spaces, and the staffing and other costs needed to keep the doors open, the collections protected, and the visitor experience meaningful.

The financial planning process outlined in this chapter is only the beginning of the planning work that is needed to ensure that the museum will be operationally sustainable. The result of this process will be rough-order-of-magnitude (or "ballpark") operational-cost estimates for the revenues generated by ticket sales, donations, memberships, or endowments and the expenses for staff and other operating costs. These initial projections are needed in order to estimate the spaces that will be included in the museum's space program and the resulting preliminary capital budget. These operating projections are also used to test fundraising goals with potential donors as you begin to build the foundation for a capital campaign. The financial projections should continue to evolve and become more detailed as the architectural, exhibit, and other planning work moves forward. It may be useful to bring in an economic feasibility consultant to help with this phase of the planning work.

As you begin, keep in mind that every museum is unique. Staffing and operational costs will vary substantially based on each museum's distinct activities and experiences. For some museums, particularly those with similar business models—like children's museums, community science centers, and many historic house museums—projections based on comparisons may seem to be relatively straightforward. But keep in mind that even very similar museums can have significantly different operations. A children's museum that has a location adjacent to a busy shopping area is likely to have higher paid visitation and higher facility costs than a similar museum in a less-accessible part of town. Identifying and adjusting for these factors is an important part of this phase of planning. Recognizing that operating costs vary substantially for different types of museums, we find it best to keep preliminary operating budgets simple. There are so many variables and "what-ifs" at this stage of planning that a primary goal is to assure the museum's staff and potential funders that the overall assumptions are broadly reasonable and responsible.

RULES OF THUMB

Before digging into the budget process, here are some rules of thumb for operational planning based on patterns we have seen:

- Staffing costs are typically 50 to 60 percent of a museum's operating budget.
- HVAC, energy, and maintenance costs typically run around 10 percent of the overall operating budget.
- While routine building repair and maintenance is typically included in a museum's operating budget, many nonprofits count on fundraising to pay for major repairs, like a new roof or HVAC upgrades.
- Marketing costs range from 1 or 2 percent up to about 10 percent of the overall expense budget. Destination museums are at the high end, and Curatorial Museums are at the low end of these estimates.
- Museums that expect to depend on earned revenue (such as admissions and event rentals) should bring an economic-feasibility consultant on board earlier in the process to help in right-sizing the facility, the exhibitions, and its operations. Museums with solid endowments and a reliable donor base may not require the same level of economic analysis.
- A museum's "cost per visitor" can be two to three times what visitors actually pay at the admission desk. The balance is made up from other sources, including donations and endowments.
- The gift shop and café should be considered amenities, not profit centers.
  - Gift shops typically do cover their own costs, but little more, once staffing is included. With a carefully curated product mix, gift shops can also be an important part of the visitor experience.
  - Museum cafés don't cover their own costs, much less return a profit for smaller museums with attendance less than 100,000 visitors per year. Even then, slow weekday visitation can make it hard to cover costs. Self-serve packaged foods available at the gift shop are the easy solution to a guest's need for a snack.
- The number of staff positions and associated operating costs will scale primarily in relation to earned revenue, but it will also vary in part by the space available for the museum's activities and experiences.

PROJECTING REVENUE

A carefully considered revenue projection underpins a sustainable operating model that, in turn, provides the necessary funds to welcome visitors, update exhibits, offer programs, and care for collections. Understanding a museum's sources of revenue provides a baseline for determining what the museum can afford for staff and other operating expenses. Knowing how much money has come in, or is likely to come in, also provides a limit on how much can be spent to support the museum's work.

Generating operating revenue is often a museum director's single biggest challenge, and, sometimes, a constant worry. Dependable revenue sources underpin the number and types of staff that can be hired, the number of exhibits and programs that can be offered, and, indirectly, the size and type of buildings that can be built. If you are looking to expand or reshape an existing museum, you may be able to develop and adjust your operating budget relatively easily based on your current budget and your experience, working to understand your future constituents. If the project is a new museum that will depend substantially on earned or donated revenue, it would likely be valuable to hire an economic-feasibility consultant and/or a fundraising-feasibility consultant (being sure that either of these comes with a track record of successful museum projects) to assist with projecting earned revenue or donations. Projected revenue is the foundation upon which the museum is built, and as such, it deserves careful thought and analysis.

Sources of Revenue

Different museums have many different sources of revenue. It is sometimes suggested that the "ideal" museum revenue mix is one-third earned (admission and gift shop), one-third "unearned" (memberships, donations, and grants—which are earned in their own ways—and one-third endowed (typically with a 4 percent draw on the endowment fund). While this "ideal" mix sounds appealing, our experience is that revenue models align more closely with the type of museum than they do with an arbitrary formula. Destination Museums (major Halls of Fame and the like) typically have the greatest percentage of earned revenue (50 to 90 percent), largely from admission and events. Curatorial Museums typically depend on endowment income or support from a much larger organization, often a university, for more than 80 to 90 percent of their support. Community Museums have the most diverse revenue streams, with an emphasis on recurring memberships and annual donations linked to exhibits, programs, events, and/or special interests, adding up to 50 to 60 percent of their revenue. These percentages can provide an initial check on your preliminary revenue estimates. While the examples here are simple, revenue and expense projections can be complex. Enlisting the help of another museum director, an economic consultant, or a board member experienced working with other nonprofits will provide valuable backup for your efforts.

A Note on Not-for-Profit Revenue Streams

As we begin to discuss revenue, it is important to note that not-for-profit museums differ from for-profit businesses primarily in their sources of revenue. While for-profit businesses rely on product sales and services, nonprofit museums are likely to depend on a wide array of revenue sources, with, as we have seen, distinctly different sources for different types of museums. A Destination Museum may well have transactional opportunities like a for-profit business—who doesn't want a T-shirt from the National Drag Racing Hall of Fame? But few Community or Curatorial Museums are likely to generate substantial earned revenue. Instead, these types of museums are more likely to gain most of their revenue from memberships, donations, and endowment.

While increasing admission prices might temporarily increase revenue, museum admission prices are set in response to the local market for cultural activities, not by the museum's need for operating funds. If a museum's prices are perceived as "too high," ticket sales and net revenue will decrease, just like they would in a for-profit business. Finding room for revenue growth can be challenging, and, for a museum, it is wise to approach revenue growth from multiple perspectives.

When looking at earned revenue, it is also important to recognize that a museum's "net cost per visitor" is often two to three times what visitors pay at the admission desk. This usually reflects the programmatic and curatorial work done behind the scenes. Many smaller and a few large museums have done away with admission charges altogether, usually projecting that increased visitation will generate increased engagement with the museum and drive membership and annual fund giving.

Creating an Initial Revenue Projection

The most reliable way to make a revenue projection for a new or transforming museum is to look at comparable museums. You may have already developed a preliminary sense of potential revenue from the benchmarking you completed in chapter 4. To begin to build your own projection, start with the museum's current budget or, for a new museum, a budget drawn from one of the comparable museums. Adjust these initial figures with potential revenue sources identified in the Logic Model or in the Activity and Experience Plan.

Many of the budget categories will be relatively easy to estimate, but projecting paid admissions is challenging—often the most difficult estimate to make in the planning process. There are few published or reference sources that provide clear guidance. And because there is little guidance, attendance is also the easiest revenue source to inflate when estimated operating costs are outstripping estimated income in the preliminary operating budget. The best way to estimate attendance realistically is with benchmarking. The challenge is in finding suitable comparables because the variables impacting attendance are many and the similarities are few. One way to approach this challenge is to offer a range of attendance possibilities with both optimistic and pessimistic projections and an operating budget based on the low estimate. Relying on a conservative estimate is a safer bet, but tagging the optimistic estimate as a "possibility" puts the value out there for the optimists without pegging the museum's future to it. In the end, if funding from admission revenue is a key budget driver, it would be advisable to bring in an economic consultant with experience with museums or nonprofits.

With attendance estimated, a little simple arithmetic will fill in the rest of the revenue projection. For example: 10,000 visitors averaging $10/visitor. Three rental events at $2,000 each. One major gala. Twelve monthly lectures. Two summer camps. Twelve hundred books. Etcetera. Etcetera. Referring to your comparables and enlisting a review by experienced museum professionals are both highly recommended as a reality check.

While there is no definitive list of the many ways museums earn revenue, typical sources include:

- Admissions
- Recurring and new memberships
- Museum shop and café sales
- Annual fund donations
- Program fees
- Special fundraising events
- Event rentals
- Support from municipal or cultural agencies or a university
- Endowment (typically at a 4 percent annual draw based on the endowment's three-year average value)

Other sources of support *not* typically included in a revenue projection may include:

- Local or regional government facility use. If your museum is in a government-owned facility, facility repair and maintenance and sometimes utilities can be included. This kind of support is not usually counted as revenue. It does, however, typically reduce facility maintenance costs, thus reducing the museum's overall expenses, and thus making other revenue sources available to cover staff or program expenses.
- Donations for special projects, perhaps including building renovations, a new exhibit, or to help build the endowment.
- Grants, typically linked to special projects, are likely to vary each year, depending on what the museum is applying for or has received.
- Restricted donations should also be noted separately since they can only be spent for specified programs or activities.

At this stage, the preliminary projection may only be a half-dozen rows. Its primary purpose will be as a gatekeeper for the expense projections. You can only budget to spend what you have projected as coming in. It will be tempting later to find ways to increase estimated revenues in order to fund favorite activities, but restraint is the mother of success in this area. Our informal assessment is that more museums have failed because of overly optimistic revenue projections than from any other cause. This preliminary revenue projection, together with its companion expense projection (described in the next section), is the straw man that will be adapted, adjusted, and fine-tuned throughout the rest of the planning project. This projection will also be important in right-sizing the building and critical in helping potential funders to understand that the museum will be able to operate successfully.

PROJECTING EXPENSES

Museum expenses fall into two broad categories: staffing and operations. Staffing is nearly always the largest expense, typically making up 50 to 60 percent of overall expenses. Other operating costs make up the remainder. The specific breakdown of operating expenses varies widely by the type of museum.

Staffing

Staffing is both the largest and most malleable expense category in a museum's operating budget. We begin to project expenses by focusing on the staff positions associated with the tasks identified in the Activity and Experience Plan (primarily exhibits, programs, and collections) and other necessary positions (possibly drawn from the comparables), including leadership, administration, marketing, fundraising, and facility maintenance.

Identifying Staffing Needs

The planning team has already identified staffing needs in the Activity and Experience Plan. Now we will pull together these needs to develop the first part of the staffing plan. Use Template 8.1 as a guide to list the needed positions. This table will eventually be the basis for the staffing section of the museum's projected operating budget. Both new and established museums should complete the assessment described in this section as it includes operational positions that are not likely to be included in the Activity and Experience Plan.

Template 8.1 Staffing Assessment Table

Position	FTEs	Salary	Benefits	Notes
Total Positions	Total FTEs	Total Salary	Total Benefits	

The first step is to list the positions identified in each section of the Activity and Experience Plan to clarify the positions that your museum needs to implement the plan. An education manager or education director position demonstrates how this might play out at different museums. At a small museum, or one that offers very few education programs, the education manager may not be a full-time role. Instead, the duties might be part of another position, like public programs or exhibits manager. At a larger museum, or one that offers a regular schedule of education programs, the position may be full-time or have multiple part-time team members reporting to a supervisor. Look closely at your Activity and Experience Plan to determine how much staff effort is required to develop and present the programs outlined there. It may be helpful to include short (one-paragraph) job descriptions for the new positions to help clarify the needed skills and time required.

Staffing and Operational Needs

Adding Operational Staff

Next, add operational staff from areas not included in the Activities and Experiences Plan. These may include leadership and administration, finance, facilities, membership, development, security, and others—areas that are key to the museum's success but are not typically included in the logic model. For existing museums, staff are likely to know where the gaps might be and can add needed positions relatively easily. For new museums, comparables are again your best source. Add these missing positions to your staff list at levels appropriate for your museum. For example, a large museum might have, in addition to curatorial and program staff, an executive director, a deputy director, a director of finance, and a director of development, all with their own direct reports. A small museum might see the director also acting as the primary development, marketing, and curatorial staff, with one other staff member responsible for managing all the operations, including finances, HR, facilities, and similar activities, with no direct reports.

Full-Time, Part-Time, and Seasonal Staff

The next step is to consider the allocation of time for full-time, part-time, and seasonal staff. Take a second look at all the activities and programs that require a specific position, and consider the time required to plan, market, and clean up after exhibits, programs, and other activities, not just the time spent presenting them. Is the position best full-time? Part-time? In between? Also consider seasonality. A museum located in an area where the population swells seasonally (Cape Cod in the summer, or Florida in the winter) might not need the same level of staff during the off-season. Similarly, the number of education staff needed might vary between the school year and the summer season. Should a position be full-time during the busy season and part-time in the off-season? Strictly seasonal? Make sure to note both seasonality and full-time/part-time on the position list, with an estimated number of hours or estimated FTE percentage for anyone not full-time.

Volunteers and Interns

Next, consider the role of interns and volunteers. If your museum already has a well-established intern or volunteer program, how do these positions supplement staffing? While interns may be temporary, they should be included on the staffing plan because they are likely to be performing substantive tasks that provide support to programs and operations. Ideally, interns should help the museum accomplish tasks that might not be completed otherwise and have direct benefit to priority constituent groups. Importantly, as a matter of equity, interns who will work at the museum for a scheduled amount of time should be included as paid staff, not as volunteers. Providing interns with a stipend, housing, or other benefits is a critical way to support the diversity of future museum professionals and promote equity within the field.

For some museums, it may be desirable to fill some staffing needs with volunteers. For example, volunteers increase the capacity for managing occasional large events. Include these roles volunteers fill on your staffing plan so you can see how operational tasks are managed. Does the museum rely mostly on staff? On volunteers? If there is a heavy reliance on volunteers for day-to-day operations, it may be worth considering if it is time to add staff to support volunteer activities in that area. While volunteers are wonderful, they can be unreliable. They may age out, develop other interests, or become less available and leave the museum scrambling. Balancing the number of staff and volunteers managing day-to-day operations will give the museum more stability and continuity, while retaining the connection to the community that volunteers offer. Be sure to also consider the role of a volunteer and/or intern coordinator. If your museum relies on volunteers or interns, having a position dedicated to recruiting, managing, and supporting these individuals can become a necessity.

Existing Staffing Review

A staffing review helps to understand the roles the current staff members take on, irrespective of their position descriptions. This review can help the museum make choices about adding new staff. To complete the review, gather your museum's current staff list or organizational chart and salary information for each position, then ask the following questions:

- Are there positions that have changed over time and no longer match their job descriptions?
- Are there positions that would be more effective with more or fewer hours?
- Are positions compensated fairly? That is, does your museum offer a wage that is commensurate with the person's duties and experience?
- Are there people doing work outside of what is typical for their position?
- Have duties accreted on to a position based on that person's skill, not necessarily their formal job responsibilities?

The same staffing template (Template 8.1) may help you organize and review this information.

As you look at the duties being performed in each position, also consider the salary for the position. Museums are notorious for both low pay and for adding responsibilities without adjustments in pay. Increasingly, the museum field has begun to discuss these challenges, and why they are detrimental to any museum's health and longevity. The low pay, sometimes described as a "passion tax," makes the field inaccessible to many who need higher-paying jobs, particularly in expensive areas. Low pay also hampers efforts to grow the diversity of people working in museums. Likewise, the number of duties a position is expected to fulfill can lead to burnout. As your museum is planning for the future, this is a good time to think about the measures you can take to make sure pay and benefits match the expectations of a similar "for-profit" job, the cost of living in the area, and standards within the field. The museum will see dividends in better staff morale, less turnover, and the ability to select from a larger pool of potential candidates for open positions.

Succession Planning

A staffing review is also the time to consider positions that are no longer as effective or necessary. Perhaps there is a part-time position tasked with managing a program or activity that the museum no longer offers or offers on a reduced scale. Could that position be shifted to cover different needs the museum has today? Likewise, this is a good time to think about succession planning. Are there staff members who are expected to leave the museum in the next few years? If so, think about the job description of their positions. Are they still a good fit for the museum's needs? What kinds of skills or traits would make a new hire most effective? These staffing changes are a good opportunity to adjust positions as needed. And thoughtful succession planning positions the museum to be prepared to advertise the position when it becomes vacant and leaves the staff down a position for as short a period as possible. Succession planning may also be important when considering interns and volunteers at your museum. Do they play a big part or a small part in operations? Are there things that would not get done without dedicated volunteers or an annual summer intern? If these positions are doing critical work, consider whether the position or responsibility should be changed to a paid staff position to ensure continuity and that key tasks get done.

The Initial Staffing Model

The list you have developed represents the ideal staffing model for the museum based on the constituents it serves, the activities and experiences offered, and the operational support that is needed.

Examine the model with your museum's DEAI work in mind. Are the positions, both existing and new, equitably compensated? How can the museum support and increase diversity within staff? How else does the staffing model support DEAI work? Again, if the model is out of alignment with the museum's DEAI work, it is important to take the time to assess why and make changes so that both the plan and the DEAI work can be successful. Keep in mind that this first-round staffing projection may be aspirational. Investing in staff will be critical to making the new programs and facility changes successful. But growing a museum's staff also means growing its revenue sources. If funding is not available, the museum will need to operate with lower staffing levels and less-ambitious programming. The detailed analysis you have developed will help to inform the hard decisions that may be necessary.

Operating Costs

While salaries and benefits will typically be the museum's largest expenses (usually over 50 percent of the operating budget), understanding other operating costs is also essential. Unfortunately, there is no simple model for projecting operating costs; they will vary significantly depending on the type of museum and its facilities. A children's museum may have few collection-storage costs, while collection storage could be a significant part of an art museum's budget. Some museums may need specialized vehicles to transport things ranging from paintings to canoes; others will have costs associated with frequent exhibit turnovers; others will change exhibits rarely. Still others may have facility costs covered by another organization, as is often the case with municipal museums. As such, every museum needs to align its own operating budget to its own priorities and realities. The following categories are typical but will vary depend on the specifics of each museum's activities, experiences, and operations.

- Visitor services
- Temporary exhibits
- Collection conservation and care
- Public programs
- Education programs
- Office expenses
- Travel and meetings
- Marketing and advertising
- Accounting and finance
- IT systems and software
- Utilities
- Security
- Off-site storage space
- And dozens of other categories

Museums that are currently operating and planning for an expansion can look at their current operating budget to determine how operating costs might change. Then, the planning team needs to consider whether the areas of greatest spending are in alignment with the new priorities, activities, and programs being developed in the museum's planning. If the plan prioritizes expanding the temporary exhibit program, then money likely needs to be added to the exhibit and marketing budgets, and it might be prudent to consider increasing the public-programs budget to support additional programs around the exhibits. Similarly, will changes to operations incur new costs? For example, increasing open hours to support public access to temporary exhibits will also require additional staff time to keep the building open. Or will changes result in cost savings? For example, a new addition may allow the museum to store all of its collections on-site, thus eliminating the rent for an off-site storage unit.

New museums will need to begin the work of developing a target operating budget, recognizing that it often takes three to five years of operations for a new museum to settle into typical attendance, revenue, and expense patterns. Best practice is for the museum to budget for higher staffing and operational costs during the first year or two of operations. Attendance at a new (or newly renovated) museum is typically higher due to public excitement. These additional startup costs usually go down in the following years. The operating projections developed in this section will, in most cases, be only a preliminary outline. As the planning moves forward and additional details, resources, and constraints are understood or reimagined, the museum's projected revenues and expenses will grow (and shrink). The planning team, in consultation with the leaders of each department, will have to make thoughtful preliminary estimates about appropriate budgets for each department and update those estimates multiple times as the planning in other areas becomes more detailed.

The exercises in this chapter are intended to help museums assess their staffing needs and other operational costs so that they can understand the impacts of making changes to who they serve and the activities and experiences that support those existing and new constituent groups. In the next chapter, we will consider how a museum's facilities will also need to grow and change to support these new constituents, activities, and experiences.

9

Facility Planning

In this chapter, we begin to unpack the facilities column of the logic model. As in chapter 8, the needs of a new museum versus an established museum differ significantly. The first part of this chapter will focus on new museums and the kinds of questions to ask to best determine the facilities a new museum is likely to need. The second part of the chapter will focus on conducting facility assessments at established museums and how to align the results of the assessment with the facility needs identified in the logic model. If you are reading this with trepidation, thinking, "I'm not an architect, engineer, or even all that skilled with a tape measure!" don't worry, the only math you will need you learned in fourth grade.

Math aside, a note of caution. As we prepare to dig into the detailed planning, it will be tempting to bring an architect on board. Architects know buildings, and you need a building, or modifications to an existing building. Why not have an architect on the team right from the beginning? Because while architects may know buildings, they most often don't know museums. And because they think visually, they may be tempted to start designing before the whole team fully understands the parameters of the project, particularly the back-of-house spaces needed to support the activities and experiences outlined in the previous chapters. Architects need to have a fully developed space plan in order to best to understand the unique spaces needed for any museum project. There is little one-size-fits-all aspects involved in the museum planning and design business. A clear, articulate, and detailed facility plan is your best tool (and defense) in the epic collaboration that will become your museum's architectural design process.

On the other hand, it is worth noting that while it is often best to wait to hire an architect until you have a clear sense of your facility needs, it may be helpful to bring on other types of experienced help at this point in the project. In this case, a space planner with direct experience planning your type of museum can be an excellent investment. They will know what works and what doesn't, what should be added and what could be deleted in "right-sizing" your space plan and then fitting it to the budget. This and other potential consultants who may be able to help will be described at length in chapter 10.

NEW MUSEUMS: ESTABLISHING FACILITY NEEDS AND PRELIMINARY BUDGETS

All the previous planning work has been leading up to this point: a facility-needs assessment. The facility-needs assessment for a new museum has five main components:

- Developing a preliminary space-needs outline
- Estimating preliminary construction costs

- Developing a preliminary capital budget
- Setting site-selection criteria
- Planning for future growth and change

Developing a Preliminary Space-Needs Outline

Using Resource 9.1, Preliminary Museum Space List, as a starting point, and your team's experience working with other museums, make a list of all the spaces needed, their principal attributes, and a best guess at their associated square footage. Be sure to include back-of-house spaces for offices, meeting rooms, curatorial needs, exhibit production, collection storage, maintenance, and administration. Meet with your team members to discuss possible current and potential future needs and add these with notes to your worksheet. Circulate the first draft to the planning team and update as necessary. Don't worry too much about the overall total at this point. It is good to let people dream a little at the beginning of the process.

When the list of spaces seems largely complete (if likely a little ambitious), add up the space needs for all the listed areas to get what is called the Net Usable Area of the building, often just referred to as "Net Area," or sometimes as "Net Square Feet" (NSF). This is the amount of usable area inside the walls of the building. The NSF does not include the space taken up by walls, hallways, stairs, elevators, and so on. We plan for these areas by applying a "grossing factor" to the Net Area. This can vary anywhere from 25 to 40 percent of the Net Area, but we typically start with 30 percent and adjust up and down as the space planning evolves. The result is an estimate of the building's Gross Square Feet (GSF), or Gross Area, which can be used in budgeting.

To check your initial work, pick a museum from one of your benchmarks and either contact the museum to ask its Gross Area in square feet, or, if that amount is not publicly available, estimate its area using its footprint on Google maps. To estimate the Gross Area, multiply the footprint by the number of levels in the building. If possible, be sure to also solicit ideas and feedback from benchmark museum staff. Even with input from the other museums, this will be a very rough estimate, but at this point, being in the right ballpark is all we need.

Outdoor space needs are also important. It can be difficult to estimate the size of these spaces at the beginning of the planning process, but it is still important to identify the need. Parking is likely the most important component. An easy way to estimate parking needs is to look at your estimated daily visitation, then divide it by 2.2. (A commonly used metric is that, on average, one car brings 2.2 visitors.) Be sure to add space for employee parking and consider overflow needs for larger museum events. Landscaping, pedestrian circulation, outdoor event spaces, sculpture gardens, and other uses will vary depending on the site, if it is known. Draft a list of these potential needs and do your best to ascribe estimated area to them. This first draft is bound to be, at best, an approximation, but it will provoke awareness and ongoing discussion about the spaces needed and how big they should be, as well as help to pinpoint any issues and concerns. That type of discussion is excellent preparation for conversations with the architect and landscape architect, when they bring their knowledge and experience to the project.

With your Preliminary Space Needs Outline in hand, it's time to return to your Logic Model and your Activity and Experience Plan. Look at the facility column for each of the prioritized groups. How do they compare with your outline? Are any spaces missing? Do the same thing with the Activity and Experience Plan, with a particular focus on the activities and experiences that serve your most important constituents. This comparison will make sure that the needs you have identified early in the planning process are clearly expressed in the Preliminary Space Needs Outline.

Estimating Preliminary Construction Costs

The next step in planning for a new museum is to estimate the costs of construction to use as a foundation for a capital budget. This preliminary construction cost estimate is a starting point for estimates that we can continue to refine as the planning moves forward. Balancing space needs, facility construction costs, and the potential for available funding will be a continuing discussion from now through the completion of the building project.

At this point, we have an initial sense of how big the museum will be from the Preliminary Space Needs Outline and the benchmarking of similar museums. Next, we need to determine the preliminary cost of construction. At this early stage, we typically use the construction cost of locally built "Class A" buildings to get an initial estimate. Class A buildings are defined as the area's "most prestigious buildings, competing for premier office users with rents above average for the area. [Class A] Buildings have high-quality standard finishes, state-of-the-art systems, exceptional accessibility, and a definite market presence."[1] This description closely resembles the needs of most public museums. Bankers and commercial real-estate professionals should be able to provide construction cost estimates to you for Class A buildings in your local area. Likewise, using local Class A construction costs creates a more accurate preliminary estimate because construction costs vary widely across the country. Class A space in New York City can cost more than twice as much as it does in Kansas City.

Developing a Preliminary Capital Budget

Estimate the initial budget needed for museum construction by multiplying the estimated Gross Square Feet by the estimated cost of Class A office space per square foot, and you have a preliminary cost for construction of the museum building. Here is the equation:

(Gross Square Feet * Class A construction cost per SF) = estimated construction costs

Precision is not required here. Increase or decrease the Gross Area in the formula until the total is a rough-order-of-magnitude construction cost that all the stakeholders can agree is a reasonable starting place. Keep in mind that if stakeholders cannot agree on "reasonable" construction costs, the project is unlikely to get off the ground. Once generally accepted, however, this initial estimate becomes a starting point for the museum's planners as they begin to further refine the museum's spaces, estimate other related capital costs, and begin to assess fundraising feasibility.

In addition to the construction costs, a building project will also have substantial "soft costs." These soft costs can vary widely by project, and they could include a wide variety of additional costs, including:

- Landscape costs
- Architectural and engineering fees
- Other specialist consultants' fees
- Furniture, Fixtures, and Equipment (FF&E)
- Specialized collection-storage systems
- Borrowing costs (if the project requires a loan or bridge loan for completion)[2]
- Moving costs
- Staff travel expenses
- Temporary storage rental

Facility Planning

Soft costs can vary substantially depending on each project's unique parameters, but typically, they range from 25 percent of the construction costs for smaller museums to 40 percent or more for larger or more complex projects.

In addition, the project may also have site acquisition costs. Site acquisition is a wild card. Sites can range from adaptive reuse of an historic building donated to the museum to the outright purchase of a prominent and empty building site. At an early stage of planning, an estimate of 20 percent of the projected construction cost is a reasonable placeholder for site acquisition.

Many projects will also have long-term exhibit costs, including design, construction, and installation costs.[3] A modest, but still high-quality, long-term exhibit for a new nature center might cost $400 to $500/SF. Dramatic, high-tech exhibits for a significant new Destination Museum could be over $1,500/SF. The amount of long-term exhibit space within the building varies substantially depending on the museum's type and the nature of the new building. For example, an addition to an existing museum might focus on collections-storage and public-program space (as identified in the Activity and Experience Plan) and not contain any long-term exhibit space. A new museum will almost certainly have some long-term exhibit space.

One way to start thinking about the amount of long-term exhibit space is to take 20 percent of the Net Area. Then, think about the importance of long-term exhibits to your mission, oversized objects you wish to display, and any other factors, then move the number up or down. Remember, increasing the amount of space for long-term exhibits also means a substantial increase to the budget and the risk that another space in the museum may have to be smaller or eliminated altogether. Do your best to balance competing needs.

Finally, contingency funding is essential. Contingency funds are money set aside to cover the "unknown unknowns" that will undoubtedly crop up as the project advances. These might relate to permitting and compliance, costs that come in higher than expected, or even conditions or challenges uncovered after the construction begins. Contingency funds serve to cover the unexpected at all stages of the project and ensure that the project is not thrown off track at the first unforeseen financial cost. As such, it is advisable to carry at least a 15 percent contingency amount to the overall, bottom-line budget in the early stages of the project. This percentage can gradually decrease as the planning becomes more detailed and more accurate estimates can be provided.

Table 9.1 provides an example of a preliminary capital budget for three different projects with space plans of 10,000, 35,000, or 100,000 net square feet. Developing this preliminary budget is another place where it may help to have expert advice. An Owners' Project Manager (OPM) can be helpful at this stage, ideally someone with experience working with cultural projects, as they will have a clear sense of local costs. An OPM is typically engaged for the project's duration, but they can also provide short-term assistance. (See chapter 10 for more details.)

The initial Preliminary Capital Budget will grow and shrink as the planning moves forward, as donors engage and disengage, and as the economy grows or stumbles. This evolving estimate will remain a touchstone throughout the rest of the planning process.

Setting Site Selection Criteria

If a specific site has not already been designated as part of the preplanning, the next step for a new museum is to set site-selection criteria. You should know approximately how big the building will be and will have a rough estimate of the amount of land that will be needed. The planning team will use this as a starting place to develop a site assessment tool that can be used to compare potential properties that fall within the specific area where a museum is looking to build. Regardless of the museum's mission, every site assessment should first ask these two questions of any property: "Is it available right now?" and, "Is the project readily permittable with local support?" If the answer to either question is no, then there is very little purpose to reviewing the property further. No matter

Table 9.1 Preliminary Capital Budgets for Three Different-Sized Museums

	Small	Medium	Large
Net Usable Square Feet (NSF) as Calculated in the Space Outline	10,000	35,000	100,000
Grossing Factor at 30% of NSF	3,000	10,500	30,000
Total Built Area in Gross Square Feet (GSF)	13,000	45,500	130,000
Cost per square foot for Class A Office Space	$600	$600	$600
Construction Cost	$7,800,000	$27,300,000	$78,000,000
Soft costs at 25, 30, and 35% of Construction Cost	$1,950,000	$8,190,000	$27,300,000
Total Construction	$9,750,000	$35,490,000	$105,300,000
Site Acquisition Estimated at 20% of Construction	$1,950,000	$7,098,000	$21,060,000
Long-term Exhibits Medium - 7,500 SF @ $400/SF Large - 25,000 SF @ $1,500/SF	N/A	$3,000,000	$37,500,000
Subtotal	$11,700,000	$45,588,000	$163,860,000
Project Contingency @ 15%	$1,755,000	$6,838,200	$24,579,000
Total Initial Project Budget	$13,455,000	$52,426,200	$188,439,000
Rounded for Discussion	$13,500,000	$52,400,000	$190,000,000

how perfect a site might be, it is of no consequence if it is not available for purchase. Similarly, if it would be difficult to impossible to get a permit to build the desired kind of facility on the property, it is of little use assessing its suitability.

To assess potential sites, the planning team needs to develop a list of the most important criteria for the property. Some of these criteria might be specific attributes, like cost, available parking, adjacency to other cultural facilities, certain kinds of outdoors space, etc. Others might be things like permitting and zoning and the cost of building on the site. The following list outlines the overarching criteria. A sample site-evaluation worksheet is included as Resource 9.2.

1. Availability
2. Approvals
3. Impact on visitation
4. Outdoor characteristics
5. Short-term cost implications
6. Long-term cost implications

Facility Planning

Table 9.2 Sample Site-Selection Scoring Table

Available	Possible Points
The site is available under normal acquisition procedures.	30
The site may be available contingent on negotiation.	0
The site is unlikely to be available.	-30

Each of the included criteria should be assigned a potential high and low score. Scoring may be assigned arbitrarily as long as the most-important qualities have the highest number of possible points and the least important qualities the lowest. Be sure to describe what it takes to get the maximum score, a medium score, and a low score. For example, for the criteria "Available" might have the following score ranges, as shown in Table 9.2.

It is important to prioritize the criteria, because it is likely that the museum may need to compromise in some areas. For example, an art museum that is building a new education center to serve K–12 students might rate ease of bus access as a 30; space to exhibit student work might score a 20; and a dedicated outdoor area for drawing classes might rate a 10. Assigning points to each category is flexible as long as they reflect the overall importance of the category. There is no need for the assessment total to add to any specific number. In our experience, effective scoring models have had as few as 200 points and as many as 550.

Once you have established high and low scores for each category, try using the criteria on a few potential properties to see how they score and then adjust the score or criteria until they seem balanced (a very subjective assessment). To use the assessment tool, have each member of the planning team (or site-selection committee, if there is one) score each property under consideration. There will likely be variation in scores, reflecting how different team members value different criteria and have different perceptions of the property. That is okay. The role of the assessment process is to provoke discussion and build consensus around the ways that different properties meet the project's articulated needs and requirements and the ways they might compromise the museum's planning, design, and activities and experiences. The planning team can then develop consensus around what is most important to identify and choose the best available property.

Planning for Future Growth and Change

Last of all, be sure to leave future museum leaders with options for growth and change. As the museum matures, it is likely that it may have different or expanded needs than the ones the planning team is tackling today. While it is hard to know what those needs will be, allowing for flexibility in use of space and leaving room for expansion will spare the museum growing pains in the future. This can be especially important once you are working with an architect. Early in the design process, be sure to ask them to show you how future expansions might fit on the site and how it might connect with the existing building. Architectural design is exciting, but it is important that the team understands what future options might be and makes decisions that will position the museum effectively for future growth and change.

ESTABLISHED MUSEUMS: CONDUCTING A FACILITY ASSESSMENT

While the space needs analysis and the budgeting tasks outlined in the previous section are important for both new and existing museums, existing museums have additional challenges when considering how to grow most successfully. A new museum is a kind of blank canvas. The planning team has few constraints other than funding. An existing museum must be much more thoughtful about how to grow and change most successfully. This section outlines some of those challenges.

The preliminary facility assessment for established museums process outlined here is simple, and it is intended to give you a baseline understanding that will guide you during future conversations with architects, engineers, and designers. The purpose of the facility assessment is twofold. First, you need to understand how much space is in your current facility and what it is used for. Second, you need to assess how well the space meets the museum's current and anticipated future needs as outlined in your work from the previous chapters. To begin, see if there are any measured drawings, blueprints, or floor plans of your museum. If you're not sure, talk to your facilities lead or your disaster-response team, who may know where these documents are. If you don't have access to these, don't worry—you can take measurements and draw simple floorplans yourself. Or, if funding is available, many firms now offer digital scanning of existing buildings and can produce detailed architectural drawings of a building in as little as a few days. These can be useful throughout the planning process. Either way, Template 9.1 provides one way to organize the space inventory. For the initial assessment, we recommend limiting the work to the staff on the planning team, as they will have a much more nuanced understanding of space than the board members. If measurements are required, work with one or two other members only. Many hands do not improve the quality of the measurements.

Template 9.1 Facility Assessment Table

Floor	Room Number/ Name	Purpose	Size	Works	Doesn't Work	Recommended Changes

Your first step will be to enter basic data about each space into the template. If you are working from plans, enter the room number and/or name, floor, size (in square feet), and purpose. Once you have entered all the rooms in your museum into the assessment table, assemble the staff members on the planning team for a walkthrough to assess the spaces. Give plenty of time for discussion and weigh the merits of conducting it when the museum is open versus closed. If you need to measure, it will be easier to do so when you are closed; on the other hand, being in the spaces when visitors and other users are present may give you better insight into what works and what doesn't about the space. If you are measuring, assume each room to be a square or a rectangle; don't worry about accounting for odd bump-outs, closets, window seats, or other irregularities. Your goal here is to get an approximate size. Then, take a hard look at the room or space and describe what "works" or "doesn't work." The following are some characteristics of spaces that work and don't work:
Spaces that work are . . .

- Universally accessible/follow universal design principles.
- Easily accommodate of the number of people who typically want to use the space.

Facility Planning

- In good working order/operable (for example, all the sinks work in the bathroom).
- Usable at all times of day and year (if indoor).
- Adjacent to related or support spaces (for example, collection processing is next door to collection storage; an area for charging museum tablets is located behind the visitor reception desk).
- Effective at creating a logical flow through the museum for both front-of-house/visitor-experience and back-of-house activities.

Spaces that don't work . . .

- Are missing elements that make them functional; for example, a classroom space lacks sinks for wet clean-up, forcing the education staff to do clean-up in the staff kitchen or public restroom.
- Have design challenges; for example, an office is not usable in the afternoon because of the strength of the sun coming in from an adjacent clear-story window.
- Are the wrong size. (Note that spaces that are too big can be just as difficult as spaces that are too small.)
- Have the wrong setup or furnishings for the use; for example, a classroom may be the right size for an adult class, but the child-scale tables are uncomfortable for adults.
- Are hard to find within the museum.
- Are far away from related spaces.
- Have the wrong adjacencies; for example, a classroom that hosts noisy activities is next to the director's office or conference room.
- Lack infrastructure (internet connection, projector, reliable electricity, etc.).
- Are not universally accessible.

Do your best to be critical and view the space with fresh eyes. Be cognizant of ways in which you or your staff have been "making things work." Sometimes these efforts do make a space work; other times, they are a struggle every day. For any attribute identified as "doesn't work," make notes in the recommended change column. Be as specific as possible here. Instead of saying "too small," note that a required piece of equipment doesn't fit in the room, or the room has capacity for twelve and typical group sizes are twenty-five. Likewise, instead of saying, "furniture not aligned with use," state: "Elementary groups struggle to use three-legged stools without falling over." Feel free to also note improvements for spaces that do work—sometimes additional changes will make them even better. For an example of what this assessment might look like in a museum classroom, see Table 9.3.

With your facility assessment in hand, it's time to return to your Logic Model with prioritized constituents and your Activity and Experience Plan. Look at the facility column for each of the prioritized groups. How do they compare with your assessment? What spaces do you already have? What spaces could you have with some small changes? What spaces are missing altogether? Do the same thing with the Activity and Experience Plan, with a particular focus on activities and experiences that serve your most important constituents. Combine your findings from the plan and the logic model,

Table 9.3 Sample Assessment of a Museum Classroom

Floor	Room Number/ Name	Purpose	Size	Works	Doesn't Work	Recommended Changes
1	102/Classroom A	Multipurpose classroom and meeting space	200 SF	Pleasing view from windows	• Too small • No storage	• Add larger classrooms, at least 400 SF each • Add education storage area

then compare them to your facility assessment. This comparison will provide a basis for thinking about facility change.

Upon the completion of these comparisons and evaluations, museums typically fall into two general outcomes:

1. The current facilities generally match with the needs identified in the Logic Model and Activity and Experience Plan, or small-scale changes, like changing the use of a space or adding a seasonal tent, could bring facilities and plans in alignment.
2. The current facilities are not in alignment with the needs identified in the logic model and Activity and Experience Plan, and significant changes, including the possible construction of new facilities, would be required for alignment.

If your museum falls into the first category, facilities may play a smaller role in your master plan. If your museum falls into the second category, more analysis may be needed, and facilities may become a larger part of the master plan. The first step is to make sure that the planning team and the museum's board both place a high priority on serving the constituent groups that would be driving significant facility change. Make sure this commitment is there from both the planning team and the board, because large-scale facility changes will likely require a commitment to a capital campaign. A new facility might also require the museum to relocate or acquire additional property. This discussion can provide an important test to the prioritization of constituents: Do the constituent priorities hold once the realities of updating the facility are considered? It may be easier and more effective to prioritize different constituent groups.

Of course, taking risks like this is critical to keeping nonprofits on mission and serving their constituents. Risk is acceptable as long as there is agreement that it is taking the organization toward opportunities and serving constituent groups that extend its mission. All facility changes carry some level of risk and will require capital investment, and likely, a capital campaign. Regardless of the size of the investment, it is important to start thinking about what the campaign might look like, who are the potential donors, what is the possibility of raising sufficient funds, and general board commitment to the potential project. Take this as a moment to firm up your case for why serving certain constituents well is so important—important enough to merit the effort of a capital campaign and the disruption of facility changes. Here, a fundraising-feasibility assessment may be needed, working with fundraising professionals who can help identify funding sources and give you confidence that the project is feasible from a fundraising perspective.

If the outcome of this discussion is that the required facility changes are out of reach, the planning team has two possible options: reassess the priority constituents or develop the project in phases. Breaking the project into smaller pieces may make it easier to fund, allow for proof of concept, and demonstrate success, which, in turn, may make future fundraising efforts easier. A phased approach has many benefits and does not require the museum to put its plans for serving new constituents entirely on hold. Instead, it gives the team a chance to come up with creative ways to address facility needs and demonstrate that creating permanent facility solutions has value to the museum's constituents. This will look different for each museum, but it might include some of the following:

- Borrowing or renting nearby space from other organizations, like classroom space or auditoriums.
- Repurposing space within the museum, even if it is not optimal for the activity.
- Using outdoor spaces.
- Partnering with other organizations to jointly develop exhibits and present programs.
- Taking it to the streets with exhibits and programs that engage new constituencies.

Keep in mind that if such programs are successful, you are simply delaying making necessary facility changes. This may be worthwhile if the museum wants additional demonstration that serving the new groups is working well, or, conversely, the board feels it would be advantageous to have more time to prepare for a capital campaign. However, if it seems there will not be support for future facility change or expansion, it may be unwise to begin programs if the museum may have a difficult time managing or housing them in the long term, should they become successful.

The Facility Plan is the last major piece of the master plan puzzle. One more time, look at the plan through the lens of the museum's DEAI work. Is the plan accessible, both in location and buildings? How does the museum's location connect it or set it apart from different communities? If the plan keeps the museum in its present location, is there any DEAI work to be done to improve accessibility and inclusion? Is anything about the plan out of alignment with the DEAI work? As always, taking the time to achieve alignment between the museum's DEAI work and the master planning is key to making both initiatives work for the museum.

COMPILING YOUR MASTER PLAN

The next step will be to pull together all the planning exercises completed here into one cohesive plan for your institution. The best approach is to have a richly illustrated and designed summary with lots of appendices that can be included or not depending on the intended audience. With the finished plan in hand, your team will be ready to move ahead with the project. At this point, it may be necessary to add professionals to your team. The next chapter will discuss the wide range of professionals who are useful in museum planning and building projects, and it provides recommendations for when to hire them, how to select them, and how to work with them successfully.

RESOURCE 9.1: PRELIMINARY MUSEUM SPACE LIST

The following list includes some of the spaces museums typically need. The most frequent complaint in existing museum buildings is that there isn't enough storage space. In line with that, our observation is that storage space is the first thing to go when the construction costs come in higher than expected and the design has to be amended. It is a better idea to think holistically and reduce front-of-house spaces to keep the necessary work and storage areas. Failing that, insist on a design that can be easily expanded to add either collections, program, or exhibit space. The museum's future staff will thank you.

1. Visitor Services Areas

1.1 Vestibule and Lobby	A welcoming transition and informative orientation
1.2 Reception Area	Set back from the entrance to allow for transition
1.3 Visitor Services Work Area	Office for cash handling and supplies
1.4 Visitor Services Storage	Wheelchairs, strollers, publications
1.5 Museum Shop	Easily accessed from entrance
1.6 Museum Shop Work Area	Storage area for merchandise, cash handling, and prepping merchandise for sale
1.7 Museum Café	Easily accessed from the entrance
1.8 Restrooms	Easily accessed from the entrance

2.0 Exhibition Areas

2.1 Long-Term Galleries	16'-plus ceilings; diffused natural light
2.2 Temporary Galleries	Easy to close off from public

2.3 Docent or Volunteer Area	Informal rest area and storage for personal belongings
2.4 Clean Exhibit Staging Area	Near loading dock, collection-receiving area, and freight elevator
2.5 "Dirty" exhibit staging area	Crating and uncrating and assembly area
2.6 Work Area for Exhibit Curator	
2.7 Exhibit Prep Workshop	

3.0 Collections

3.1 Collection Storage	Adequate floor loading, fire protection, and security
3.2 Collection Receiving Area	Accessible to loading dock and collection work areas
3.3 Collection Processing	Accessible to curatorial work area
3.5 Curator's Office	With space for artifact research
3.6 Assistant Curator's Office	
3.7 Registrar's Work Area	Good lighting, file storage, and multiple worktables
3.7 Collection Assistant's Workspace	Adjacent to Collection Processing

4.0 Public Program and Education Areas

4.1 Multipurpose Program Area	
4.2 Adjacent Table and Chair Storage	
4.3 Classroom(s)	Specifically designed for use by student groups
4.4 Student Lunch Space	Temporary storage for student backpacks
4.5 Auditorium	Complements 4.1
4.6 Public Program Storage	May include chairs, tables, and other items
4.7 Education Supply Storage	
4.8 Education Workspace	Program preparation area
4.9 Event or Function Space	In addition to or replacing 4.1
4.10 Warming Kitchen	Generally, a full catering kitchen is unnecessary
4.11 Office for Education Director	
4.12 Museum Educator's Workspace	Typically shared or dedicated carrels
4.13 Office for Program Director	
4.14 Office for Program Manager	

5.0 Administration and Operations

5.1 Administrative Work Areas	Consistent with chapter 8
5.2 Copy Room and Supplies Storage	
5.3 Staff and Volunteer Break Area	Simple kitchen items; may include space for volunteers to store belongings
5.4 Storage for Financial and Other Records	
5.5 Staff Restrooms	

6.0 Maintenance and Utility Areas

6.1 Loading Dock
6.2 Secure Temporary Storage
6.3 Maintenance Workshop
6.4 Maintenance Staff Offices and Work Areas

RESOURCE 9.2: SITE EVALUATION WORKSHEET

The criteria below represent sample site-selection criteria. These criteria were developed for a regional nonprofit promoting recreational opportunities. A score sheet follows the narrative list of criteria.

1. Availability

1.1 Available

30 The site is available under normal acquisition procedures.
0 The site may be available contingent on negotiation.
-30 The site is unlikely to be available.

2. Approvals

2.1 Readily Permitted

20 Land and/or building(s) have limited historic or environmental concerns, and zoning board and community have indicated support for permitting.
10 Official and neighbors are open to special zoning and other permits.
0 There is some community and zoning board support, mixed with others who are unsure and some who oppose the project.
-10 Zoning board has indicated opposition to the project.

2.2 Local Support for the Project

10 "Loud" local support exists for developing the site.
5 Public opinion is mixed; no strong feelings exist either way.
0 Public opposition to the project exists.

3. Outdoor Characteristics

3.1 Adequately Sized

30 There is enough area for current programs and future growth, with two acres or more.
15 There is enough area for current programs, with a minimum of two acres.
10 It is cramped, but has other appealing qualities, with less than two acres.
0 The location would not accommodate current programs, with less than one acre.

3.2 Open Space for Programs and Events

10 Site has several acres of open fields, with a minimum of two acres.
5 Site has at least one acre of open field.
0 Site has limited open outdoor areas, with less than one acre.

3.3 Easily Developed for Parking

10 Location has already developed parking, or has large, level spaces that could be easily converted to parking for a minimum of fifty cars.
5 Location has limited areas that could be developed for parking, for about thirty-five parking spaces.
0 Parking is significantly constrained by topography, wetlands, or other permitting issues. Total available spaces are twenty or fewer.

4. Impact on Visitation

4.1 Accessible Location

25 It is centrally located and easy to find; on a major road, defined as a state highway or numbered road.
15 The location is within five minutes of a major road.
0 The location requires taking two or more back roads from a major road.

4.2 Access to Outdoor Recreation

25 Location provides direct access to a notable river or trail system.
10 Location is nearby or a short drive away from a notable river or trail system.
0 There are no nearby trails or river access points.

4.3 Aesthetic Considerations

20 There are enticing views to and from the site, mature landscape, inviting topography, and compatible neighbors.
10 The location is well maintained with potential.
0 It is challenging to imagine the location being beautiful.

5. Short-Term Cost Implications

5.1 Existing Buildings

30 Existing buildings align with the museum's mission.
15 Some existing buildings(s) can be adapted for programs or offices.
0 There are no existing buildings, or they are not suitable.

5.2 Investment Required

30 The museum has the capital to make the location suitable, or the location already has many of the core requirements in place.
15 The museum could make the investment required with some fundraising, or the location has some core requirements in place.
0 The investment required to develop the property is substantial.

5.3 Purchase Price and Capital Budget

20 $3M or less
10 $3M-6M
0 Over $6M

6. Long-Term Cost Implications

6.1 Anticipated Maintenance Costs

20 Anticipated carrying costs will be about the same as current rent.
10 Anticipated carrying costs will be about 25 percent higher than current rent.
0 Anticipated carrying costs will be double the current rent.

6.2 Ability to Generate Revenue

30 The site has program areas suitable for event rentals and other revenue-generating programs. It also has access to recreation that could attract an outfitter as a tenant.

10 The site has program areas suitable for event rental and revenue-generating program *or* access to recreation that could attract an outfitter as a tenant.

5 The site is constrained, with limited space for rental and programs, or it lacks access to recreation, which will limit revenue possibilities.

0 The site cannot accommodate large program/event spaces, and it does not have access to recreation.

6.3 Anticipated New Staffing Costs

10 Anticipated staffing costs will be about the same.
0 Anticipated staffing costs will be about 25 percent higher than currently budgeted.

Table 9.4 Sample Site-Evaluation Score Sheet
The score identifies desirable attributes for the regional organization described in Resource 9.2. Each attribute is assigned points based on its importance. High total scores indicate a very desirable location; low scores a less desirable location or a location with challenges that will need to be overcome.

	Site A	Site B	Site C
1. Availability			
1.1 Available			
2. Approvals			
2.1 Readily permitted			
2.2 Local support for the project			
3. Outdoor Characteristics			
3.1 Adequately sized			
3.2 Open space for programs and events			
3.3 Easily developed for parking			
4. Impact on Visitation			
4.1 Accessible location			
4.2 Access to outdoor recreation			
4.3 Aesthetic considerations			
5. Short-Term Cost Implications			
5.1 Existing buildings			
5.2 Investment required			
5.3 Purchase price and capital budget			

	Site A	Site B	Site C
6. Long-Term Cost Implications			
6.1 Anticipated maintenance costs			
6.2 Ability to generate revenue			
6.3 Anticipated new staffing costs			
Totals			

NOTES

1. Building Owners and Managers Association International, "Building Class Definitions," Building Owners and Managers Association International, https://www.boma.org/BOMA/Research-Resources/Industry_Resources/BuildingClassDefinitions.aspx (accessed May 31, 2024).
2. We should note that in our experience, the single-most-common reason for a museum project to fail is borrowing to fund a building project or borrowing to complete construction when costs come in over the estimates. See chapter 10, "The Master Plan and Next Steps," for additional details.
3. Note that many museums refer to their long-term exhibits as "permanent exhibits." We prefer *long-term exhibits*, as no exhibit is truly permanent. After ten to twenty years, exhibits begin to become dated or worn and need to be updated, hence, they are long-term.

10

The Master Plan and Next Steps

At this point in the process, the planning team should have a strong understanding of its priority constituent groups; the activities and experiences that meet the needs of each of those groups; and the staffing, operations, and facilities needed to bring the new, expanded, or revitalized museum to life. All the components of the planning work developed so far should be compiled into a single document, the master plan, which all the team members can use as a source and reference during fundraising and as a foundation for detailed implementation plans for collections, exhibits, programs, operations, and architectural design. Your next steps will depend on your museum's unique circumstances, the board's readiness, and, potentially most challenging, the availability of funds for the project. In this chapter, we will outline some of the possible paths forward.

Most of these paths will require hiring a range of different consultants and experts, including fundraisers, architects, consulting curators, interpretive planners, exhibit designers, project managers, and others, all with specialized skill sets. All of these will help the museum to develop the detailed plans that will take it closer to its goals. For each group of professionals, we will note:

- Why this type of consultant might be a good next step
- What each type can and can't do to advance a project
- Specific recommendations for selecting each professional
- Suggestions for working with them effectively

Keep in mind that every project is different. Some projects may need all of the professionals outlined here; others may require only one or two. Likewise, the timing of bringing each consultant into the project will vary, depending on the project's focus, scope, and timeline. If the team isn't sure whom to hire first, do some initial outreach to possible consultants, outline the project to-date, ask them how they can help, and discuss what the best time would be to bring them into the project. This feedback is often helpful in developing a realistic schedule for each part of the project.

The kinds of professionals we will explore in this chapter include:

- Fundraising consultants, who help the museum determine how much money could be raised and the best ways to raise it.

- Space planners, who translate the museum's desired activities and experiences into a package of specific spaces and building needs that an architect can use to develop a design.
- Contract curators, who can support the museum's curatorial staffing in making decisions about future collection-storage, workspace, and research areas.
- Interpretive planners and exhibit designers, who help museums determine which stories to tell and how to effectively present those stories to visitors.
- Architects, who design the building and work with a construction company to manage building it.
- Owners' project managers, who represent the interests of the museum to the architect and construction manager throughout the process.

ON BEING A STRONG CLIENT

Before we begin, it is important to understand the value of being a strong client. The work you have done to accomplish your master plan is a first step. You know what you need and want, and you can articulate and defend the need for the spaces and activities you have planned. As a strong client, you should:

- Ask questions and then ask more questions. Fully understand every concept.
- Understand, clearly state, and state again, as often as needed, your own nonnegotiables, including space needs, site and building organization, facility types, cost, and location.
- Provide thoughtful, substantive critique to ideas, concepts, and draft plans.
- Stick to review meeting schedules to help keep the overall schedule on track.

While it is important for you to be a strong counterpart when working with any consultant, architects and exhibit designers often require additional skills to manage:

- Learn the language architects and designers use to talk about space and function. (If they tell you something is "tectonic," you are free to laugh out loud, or at least ask for an explanation.)
- Learn to read 2D design drawings to understand the utility and function of spaces. Many 3D walkthrough renderings are inspiring, but they often make it more difficult to understand spatial relationships.
- "Walk" through plans as if you were in the building. "Greet" a visitor and walk with them through the public areas. "Receive delivery" of a sensitive artifact and ensure it can get to a secure location quickly and easily without exiting the secure path.
- Rigorously defend the museum's functional needs in the face of the architect's aesthetic vision or the exhibit designer's bold ideas. Tell them these functional needs are "creative constraints" within which they need to work, even if it means the atrium is six feet shorter or there is one less interactive exhibit.
- Defend the need for adequate exhibit-preparation areas, even if it means the full-height curtain wall will be a shade less dramatic.
- Insist that the loading dock and associated areas be fully accessible for any size truck with any turning radius.
- Don't be afraid to send the architect or designer back to the drawing board multiple times. They may grumble, but in our experience, every revision makes the design team think again, and, most often, that second thought makes the design more integrated, the building more fully functional, and the museum more delightful to visit.

FUNDRAISING FEASIBILITY STUDY/FUNDRAISING CONSULTANTS

Fundraising consultants are typically brought on board to develop capital campaign-feasibility studies that estimate how much money the museum can raise in a capital campaign—a key piece of information in sizing a museum-building project. A fundraising-feasibility study assesses the potential for fundraising based on a given project or set of priorities. The report provides a range for the amount of money that a museum is likely to be able to raise for a particular project. After conducting a feasibility study, it may make sense to keep the consultant on board, especially if the museum lacks a dedicated development team, to provide expertise, coaching, and support for staff, especially the director, who will lead most of the fundraising efforts. While it is possible to hire a firm to do the fundraising for you, this approach is expensive and adds to the total amount of money you will need to raise. In our experience, the most effective campaigns are ones where the staff and board are leading the charge with support and advice from the consultants. Donors are typically more confident in saying yes to people at the organization with whom they are already familiar.

Fundraising Consultants Can:

- Conduct fundraising feasibility studies.
- Assess the overall nonprofit fundraising landscape in your region. Who is raising money for what? How much can the overall community support? Where are the most likely potential opportunities?
- Provide the planning team with feedback on the proposed project or priorities based on donor responses.
- Coach the museum's director, board, or other staff to help them prepare presentations and make asks to donors, foundations, and others.
- Develop collateral or other fundraising materials.
- Help develop events and celebrate success.

Fundraising Consultants Can't:

- Guarantee a successful capital campaign or that the museum will meet its fundraising targets.

Selecting a Fundraising Consultant

When hiring a fundraising consultant, the museum should consider the consultant's familiarity with the region, the type of projects the consultant has worked on in the past, and the consultant's overall personality/approach. It is important to select a consultant with whom the staff and board members feel comfortable working—someone they feel they can trust to coach them in making asks of potential donors. Then, consider the consultant's location and experience. Generally, consultants should work regularly in your region so they are aware of where the deep pockets are, what other campaigns or organizations are competing for available dollars, and how to best pitch to supporters and potential supporters in the area. Ideally, they should also have some experience working on cultural projects or projects similar to what your museum is seeking to accomplish. And, of course, review their past campaigns to see if they were successful!

Working with a Fundraising Consultant

To get the most out of your work with a fundraising consultant, be sure to provide detailed information about the proposed project so the consultant can present the project accurately and so they can provide feedback on approaching donors or developing fundraising collateral. If possible, it is helpful for each person to think about the most effective ways for them to be coached so the consultant can adjust their approach as needed.

SPACE PLANNERS

Space planners translate the museum's desired activities and experiences into a package of specific spaces and building needs that an architect can use to develop a design. The space planner's role is to make sure that the museum's spaces are clearly and fully articulated so the resulting design meets the museum's needs. Once a space plan is complete, the space planner will work closely with the architect during the first phases of design to make sure that space needs are being translated correctly and functional pieces of the museum, like the loading dock, aren't getting short shrift. Space planners may also assist the architect's interior designer to ensure that finishes and furniture meet the needs of the space users—child-scale furniture in the classroom for elementary learners, for example. Often, the architect will have a space planner on staff or a contract planner they use on a regular basis. Ideally, the space planner will have experience working with museums and understand their needs and requirements.

Space Planners Can:

- Provide a clear outline of the kinds of spaces needed, their adjacencies, and the specific characteristics of each space.
- Make recommendations on the placement of certain spaces within the museum.
- Provide a document that can inform rough-order-of-magnitude budgets for construction, exhibits, and other costs.
- Serve as a check on the architect to make sure initial designs truly meet the museum's needs.
- Offer advice or formal review of space allocation and specifications throughout the design process.

Space Planners Can't:

- Design the building or its systems.
- Design outdoor spaces or parking.
- Provide interpretive planning or exhibit-design services.
- Provide detailed construction or exhibit budgets.

Selecting a Planner

When selecting a space planner, look for a consultant who has demonstrated experience working with museums of the same type as yours—an art museum has very different needs from a science center. While all museums share some interchangeable parts, museums of different types have very different needs. A planner who specializes in children's museums, which have few collections, might struggle to effectively develop art storage, preparation, and curatorial areas for an art museum.

Working with a Planner

When working with a space planner, provide them with as many details as possible about current activities and the activities and experiences the planning team is envisioning. Whenever possible, have the planner meet directly with the staff who use the spaces so the planner can understand what works well about current spaces, what is challenging, or based on the staff members' professional careers, what has worked well or failed in other museums. Ask the planner lots of questions throughout the process, and have them explain why spaces are added or left out (if the museum's planning team thinks they are missing). The space planner can also be an important advocate for the museum with both architects and exhibit designers. If needed, ask the planner to help you talk to these professionals and help you make a case for certain needs or design requests.

PLANNING FOR COLLECTIONS

Collections are the intellectual foundations of many museums. But planning for them often takes a back seat to architecture and exhibit design. While there are many well-qualified consulting curators, this is an area where you are most likely to be able to rely on the museum's own collection managers or curators. They know their collection needs and can work with storage-system vendors and other service providers to plan space and storage needs. That said, it never hurts to bring in someone from outside the museum to add a different perspective. If your museum choses to work with a contract curator, we recommend the same approach for selecting and working with them as for a space planner. In either case, a few pointers from the trenches may be helpful.

Make sure that the museum's circulation system makes it possible to easily move collections behind the scenes. Ideally, there should be three discrete circulation systems:

- Collections circulation, connecting the loading dock to exhibit-prep areas and collections storage.
- Staff circulation, for administrative and front-of-house staff, connecting offices to program areas and public areas.
- Public circulation with access to emergency exits that does not compromise the other circulation systems.

Such a set of systems may be difficult to implement, especially in a single-story building, but even posing it as a requirement will prompt discussion of issues that are critical for the security and management of collections. These discussions will help the architect develop the best possible circulation given the constraints of your museum.

Other collection space–planning considerations that an architect or space planner may not consider include:

- In a larger museum, it is ideal to have two separate receiving areas, one for collections and the other for general purposes, including catering access and trash and recycling handling. Separate the art from the artichokes.
- The receiving area should have adjacent secure storage so that collections items can be delivered and stored securely until they are ready to be unpacked and processed.
- Researchers and the museum's curators will appreciate a secure space where artifacts can be brought to researchers for study. This could be a classroom-like space for a university museum or a small office with a window in the wall or door to facilitate monitoring.
- We recommend "wet" fire suppression for collections areas. So-called dry pipe systems offer the illusion of security from water leaks, but they are significantly more expensive, require more ongoing maintenance, and, ironically, may be at greater risk of leakage. In any case, reports of wet systems failing and damaging collections are few and far between.

There will be multiple other concerns for each museum's unique collection. This is an area with a particular need for a strong client. Make your voice heard.

INTERPRETIVE PLANNERS AND EXHIBIT DESIGNERS

Interpretive planners and exhibit designers support story-centric museums in determining which stories to tell and how to effectively present those stories to visitors. If your story-centric museum is planning to serve new constituent groups or change the kinds of stories on which it focuses, hiring an interpretive planner is a good next step. An interpretive planner can review the people, stories, and artifacts in your collection and archives and develop interpretive themes that will guide the development of exhibits and related programs. Interpretive themes are like guardrails: they place boundaries within the universe of themes, ideas, and stories your museum can tell so that programs and exhibits are focused on the most important content. Going forward, they provide a good test for any proposed program or exhibit—if it is not aligned with the interpretive themes, it is likely not a good use of time and resources. A story-centric museum should have a solid and compelling interpretive plan before beginning the exhibit-design process.

If your museum has an established interpretive plan already, you can move directly to hiring an exhibit designer, who will help bring to life specific stories and objects. They will determine which stories to tell, select objects to feature, and write content for wall text, interactives, and other components. They will also design the layout, the built elements, and the cases, plinths, and other furniture for exhibiting objects. Exhibit designers work on as small a scale as a single exhibit case within a museum all the way to an entire museum. If many exhibits are being redone or if your project is a new museum, working with one exhibit designer rather than spreading the work between firms is likely to produce a more cohesive effect.

Interpretive planners work closely with exhibit designers, and they often are part of the same firm. If a firm has both planners and designers, the lines between what each can and can't do may blur.

Interpretive Planners Can:

- Set the direction for the kinds of stories told at the museum.
- Make recommendations for bringing those stories to life through exhibits, multimedia, and programs.
- Suggest different interpretive and exhibit techniques.
- Draft exhibit or media content.

Interpretive Planners Can't:

- Design or build exhibits.
- Develop A/V or multimedia experiences.

Exhibit Designers Can:

- Design the space, including cases, furniture, and so on.
- Select artifacts or artwork for display.
- Select color schemes, font, and other design elements.
- Develop content, including wall and label text, A/V or media, and interactive elements.
- Prepare drawings for fabricators.

Exhibit Designers Can't:

- Set the direction or provide big-picture thinking about interpretive themes.

Selecting an Interpretive Planner or Exhibit Designer

If you don't have one already, create a staff committee specifically charged with developing the new exhibit or with steering the interpretive planning process. (Depending on your museum, involving the board may be important as well.) This group will begin the selection process and be responsible for working with the selected consultant to prepare the interpretive plan or design a new exhibit. The group will likely have a choice of both local firms and firms that work nationally. There are benefits and challenges to each approach. A nearby firm may be easier to work with informally. A regional or national firm may be a better fit for your type of museum or the challenges of telling your specific story. Overall, rather than focusing on geography, it is most important to look at how a consultant will approach the unique challenges and circumstances at your museum. Reviewing plans and designs for the consultant's prior projects will give you a sense of their general style and may help the planning team understand how a consultant approaches different kinds of museums.

While it is not equitable or appropriate to ask potential designers to provide sketch designs or plans for your space, you can still ask about their general approach, including the kinds of materials they might use, how they might engage with specific artifacts from your collection, and how they might use interactive or A/V elements. The goal is to help you understand whether or not your vision is aligned with the designer's. When talking to interpretive planners, ask what they see as the most important stories or what makes your museum unique in their eyes. If those are off-base from the project team's ideas, it is likely not a good match. Just as with other consultants, it is good to make sure personalities on both sides of the table seem well matched, and to understand how the consultant's work process aligns with the team's preferred approach or work habits and the project schedule. With all this in mind, the planning team can select a planner or designer and move forward.

The Consultant Selection Process

While personalities and communication styles are important in finding interpretive-planning and exhibit-design teams, it is also important to have a clearly defined selection and contracting process. Most museum organizations, including the American Alliance of Museums (AAM), the American Association for State and Local History (AASLH), and the Association of Science and Technology Centers (ASTC); regional museum networks, like the New England Museum Association (NEMA) and the Mid-Atlantic Association of Museums (MAAM); and others, have resources related to the process described below on their websites.

- Start your search with an RFQ (Request for Qualifications). Unlike an RFP (Request for Proposals), which asks a consultant to generate a detailed work plan and cost estimate for the work outlined in the RFP, an RFQ asks potential consultants to share their qualifications and experience with similar projects. As an RFQ does not ask for a price quote, it is easier for consultants to submit their qualifications, and you may receive a better response.[1]
- Depending on the responses to your RFQ, you can interview, select a team, and develop a contract with the selected team. Or, more likely, after informal interviews with consultants who responded to the RFQ, you will want to select four to six firms to respond to an RFP.
- Developing an RFP is a more rigorous task than developing an RFQ, primarily because an RFP involves money. Because creativity is an important resource and difficult to put a price on, we prefer to assign a preliminary budget and ask consultants to describe what they can produce within the proposed budget. This collaborative approach still helps you find the best value for your investment and sets the stage for future collaboration and budget negotiations.
- Once RFP responses are received, interview the top three or four firms and make a selection.

Working with an Interpretive Planner and Exhibit Designer

Both interpretive planning and exhibit design will likely begin with preliminary research, followed by a site visit and initial meetings with staff, stakeholders, and project leads. Often, the interpretive planner will work with the museum first to clearly define the scope and nature of the project. The completed interpretive plan can then be passed on to the design team. If the interpretive planner is part of the design team, they will work together with the design team to dig into the collections while the interpretive framework is being developed and embedded in the exhibit's concept design.

Exhibit design will most often follow the same major steps as architectural design:

- Concept design (Concept) lays out the preliminary ideas and visuals for the exhibits. This level of design is typically what is needed to produce fundraising materials.
- Schematic Design (SD) is a first draft of the design. It integrates exhibit-design concepts with the building's general layout. It typically includes floor plans, preliminary object lists, and circulation studies.
- Design Development (DD) includes 3D renderings integrated with the building. Typically, DD now includes a "fly through" model of the exhibits in the building. DD is the refined, nearly final, version of the design.
- Construction Documents (CD) provide the final, detailed design documents, and the information needed to build the exhibits. These include all the technical details for exhibit and artifact lighting, A/V integration, and integration with the building.

During each phase of the design process, the most important role for the museum's team is to provide the consultant with clear direction and feedback based on their desired project outcomes and budget limits.

ARCHITECTS

Significant changes to a museum's site or building, or the construction of a new facility, will require bringing an architect on board. For architects, a museum is an exciting opportunity. Museums seem to offer more space for architectural creativity than is possible in other building types, and architects have been known to let their imaginations run wild and propose things that are architecturally quite interesting but may lack some of the function that the museum needs. A classic example of this is Daniel Libeskind's addition to the Denver Art Museum. The design is dramatic, echoing the mountains in the distance, but it has proven to be challenging for museum operations—hanging paintings in galleries with sloping walls is just one of the building's disconnects. If one of your goals is dramatic architectural design, it is especially important to be a strong client. Be certain that you have a clear plan for the functions that must be possible in a new building, as you determined them in chapter 9, before bringing an architect to the table.

Architects will typically assemble a design team of professionals to support the project. A short list of other needed professionals may include:

- Landscape architects, who design the natural areas around the building, parking, drainage, and other exterior needs.
- Code consultants, who will make sure that the building as designed meets all applicable building, access, and fire codes.
- Engineers, including civil engineers, who will make sure that the design is structurally sound, and mechanical engineers, who will design electrical, plumbing, ventilating, heating, and cooling systems.

- Interior designers, who will select paint colors, flooring materials, furniture, and some utility lighting.
- Lighting designers, who will develop an overall lighting plan for interior and exterior spaces.
- Acoustic consultants, who will make sure that sound moves (or doesn't move) effectively, depending on a space's purpose.
- Other specialized consultants based on the project's unique needs.

What an Architect Can Do:

- Design plans for new buildings or renovations to an existing building that fully address the museum's future needs as outlined by museum staff in the master plan.
- Coordinate the building design with the exhibit designer (if needed).
- Make sure the building connects with landscape and surrounding areas appropriately.
- Suggest the best ways to integrate the museum's existing space.
- Work with lighting, interior design, acoustic, and HVAC consultants to make the spaces usable.
- Work with a landscape architect to connect outdoor spaces, including space for outdoor sculptures, classrooms, and other needs.
- Work with the Construction Manager (CM) and Owner's Project Manager (OPM) during the construction phase. (For more information on OPMs, see the section below.)

What an Architect Can't Do:

- Design exhibits.
- Directly manage actual construction.

Selecting an Architect or other Design Professional

Finding the right architect for your project can be challenging. Sometimes it seems as if architects see museums as a blank canvas on which they can express their tectonic spirit without the typical design restraints of commercial buildings. This narrow view of museum design is reinforced by the architectural and general press that celebrate a museum's outward expression with little regard for interior function. This notion of "museum as trophy" may satisfy a significant donor, but it is just as likely to frustrate the curator and exhibit teams when glass façades bring too much light into the galleries or restrooms are located on the floor directly above collection storage. Design matters. But good looks need to be balanced with enhanced function. The best design professionals will find ways to have both.

Finding the right architect begins with identifying the firms that have experience designing and building museums. Experience with other cultural buildings, like libraries, can also be helpful, but direct museum experience is highly desirable. As noted above, museums are functionally very complex buildings, and experience designing them pays off. A promise to give you "exactly what you want" is not nearly as helpful as proof that they will help you get what you need (with apologies to the Rolling Stones).

The internet, of course, is your friend here. Review the portfolios of experienced architects online and identify those with projects of similar scale to your own. If possible, visit several of these projects and talk with staff who can provide insights into both the process and the outcomes. In identifying potential firms, don't feel constrained by geography. It is great if a firm is just down the road, but museum architects often partner with local architects to divide the work. With this approach, the museum architects develop the design (concept, schematics, and design development), and the local architects develop construction documents and manage construction supervision.

The Master Plan and Next Steps

The RFQ and RFP process for architects is much like the process for exhibit design outlined above. An RFQ leads to a short list of firms invited to present to the planning committee either before or after responses to an RFP. At this point, it may be useful to bring in an owner's project manager (see section later in this chapter) to help manage the RFP and selection process and potentially continue to work with the architect to develop the design and, ultimately, begin construction.

Working with an Architect

Working with an architect can be very exciting—finally the needs and ideas are starting to come to life through renderings. Team members can see what the project might look like. At the same time, it's important not to be swept away by excitement or fancy renderings. Make sure the museum is still getting what it needs out of the proposed building. Be careful not to compromise on aspects that serve key constituent groups. It is well worth taking the extra time now, even if it means creating some conflict, to make sure the final design addresses the challenges the museum was facing that prompted the project. Invest the time in reviewing the design. Planning is cheap; building is expensive!

What to Expect from Various Design Stages

Design is typically broken into Concepting/Conceptual Design, Schematic Design, Design Development, and Construction Documents. Each stage represents specific milestones in the project. The following descriptions have been adapted from *Planning Successful Museum Building Projects*.[2] This section is intended as an overview only.

- Concepting/Conceptual Design is the first phase in the design process. It develops the general layout of the building, the systems that will support it, and, of course, what the building will look like. Products from this phase include floor plans, site plans, simple renderings/narrative descriptions, descriptions of building systems, initial cost estimates, and similar materials describing the project. Conceptual materials often form the basis of a capital campaign. Conceptual design is typically about 5 percent of the total design budget.
- Schematic Design takes the concept design and begins to add detail to major components so that you can assess how specific spaces will perform. This phase will allow you to refine the project budget further. Schematic Design is typically about 15 percent of the design budget.
- Design Development takes the Schematic Design documents and develops them in three dimensions with further detail, including materials, systems, and other specifications. Design development completes about 45 percent of the design budget.
- Construction Documents reflect the complete design and provide the level of detail needed to construct the building or complete a renovation. The construction documents are what you will use to go to bid with a contractor or construction firm and inform the final budget for the project. They typically represent 35 percent of the design budget.

Design, Fundraising, and Debt

It is important to do a conservative reassessment of your preliminary fundraising feasibility at the completion of the Conceptual Design phase. Moving forward with Schematic Design without having firm commitments for at least 50 percent of the funding necessary to build that design is unwise. Should there be economic changes or other circumstances that affect the museum's ability to raise the needed funds, the preliminary concepts can be much more easily downsized if they haven't been fleshed out to the next level of design.

If you cannot meet your fundraising targets, it's time to reassess. Why are you falling short? Is it because the concept isn't compelling? Because your pool of funders is tapped out? Is the project too ambitious? Too conservative? Whatever the case, it is time to reflect and redesign to align the design with the resources you have rather than saddling the museum with debt. While it may sting (and cost additional architectural fees), the additional fees are paltry compared to the cost of building. Finding a workable solution now will make sure you get your most important needs met with the funds you have.

Budget shortfalls may also tempt the museum to value-engineer its way out of a shortfall. Value Engineering (VE) is a common method to cut costs by lowering the quality of finishes, specifying cheaper systems, or other means. VE is a useful process and one that can provide important cost savings. At the same time, be careful not to use it as the only tool to reduce cost, lest you end up with a building that is less functional on multiple fronts. If drastic cost reductions are needed, it's time to reconsider both site and size instead of value engineering. Remember, even if you incur additional planning and design costs, these are small compared to construction costs.

Last, it is important to offer words of caution about debt. Too often, we have seen museums encouraged to take out loans to finance a construction project when fundraising falls short or stalls. Funders are seldom inspired to donate to pay down debt. That debt payment then becomes an operating cost for the museum, often a crippling, and sometimes fatal, outcome. The reality is that it is exceptionally hard to fundraise for a building that has already been completed. Funders know that a capital campaign just happened, and you have a brand-new building. That reality makes it hard to see a need for more money. We strongly urge museums to avoid construction debt, even if it means deferring the project or cutting back the program substantially. The only exception to this rule is the use of a bridge loan to cover funds already pledged but not yet received.

OWNERS' PROJECT MANAGER

Beyond the consultants and professionals outlined above, the museum may also want to add a person to their own staff who can manage the project and serve as an advocate for the museum's needs. Building projects are complex, and surveys show that most museum directors only experience one major building project in their careers.[3] So, if you feel less prepared than you would like to be, you're not alone!

One solution to this challenge is to hire an Owners' Project Manager (OPM). OPMs are knowledgeable about construction and project management. Their role is to represent the interests of the owner to the architect and construction manager throughout the process. The OPM is selected by the museum and remains fully "on your side" to help you understand the process and make the best decisions based on the information or choices being presented to you. Retaining an OPM may not be needed for a small project, but it is certainly advisable for major projects.

What an OPM Can Do:

- Coordinate the construction and design process for the museum.
- Act as the museum's representative and advocate.
- Communicate decisions on behalf of the museum.

What an Owner's Representative Can't Do:

- Design or redesign a building.
- Construct or manage the construction of the building.
- Act independently.

Selecting an OPM

Many firms, large and small, offer OPM services. Experience working with museums or cultural buildings is not as important for this role as it is with other roles, but it is still valuable. You may want to approach your architect or other nearby museums that have recently completed a construction project for recommendations. The OPM is the museum's trusted advocate and guide in managing the building process. It is critical that the museum team select an individual who can explain things in nontechnical terms and is easy to communicate with.

Working with an OPM

Clear, frequent communication is the key to an effective relationship with your OPM. The OPM is the go-between for the construction manager and the museum team. They cannot do that effectively if they are not in regular contact with the museum team. The museum team should meet at least weekly with the OPM and be prepared to meet more often or on short notice if the project hits an unexpected challenge.

Other Staffing Considerations

In addition to the owner's representative, some museums may decide that having a temporary staff position dedicated to managing the construction project and keeping the director and other key staff and board members in the loop is helpful. This person might be reassigned internally as a temporary role, or the museum might choose to hire someone with museum experience specifically for the term of the construction project. For large projects or large museums, having this role may be very helpful to ensure that internal communication and daily impacts of construction are understood by all.

At this point, it is time for the museum's planning team to chart its own course, selecting additional consultants and choosing its first action steps. Your museum's path will be distinct from every other museum based on the resources available, local conditions, and the goals set for the planning process. There will be uncertainties and difficulties as you begin, as you continue, and even as you see the finish line. Despite the potential challenges, the museum will persevere because your master plan provides a solid, yet flexible, foundation that is grounded in an in-depth understanding of and deep concern for your constituents' interests, needs, motivations, and desires.

NOTES

1. For more on the debate between issuing an RFP or and RFQ, see Barbara Punt, "To RFP or Not to RFP: That Is the Question," *Exhibition* (Spring 2019), 68–76.
2. Walter L. Crimm, Martha Morris, and L. Carole Wharton, *Planning Successful Museum Building Projects* (Lanham, MD: AltaMira Press, 2009), 72–73.
3. Ibid., 11.

11

What Really Happens Next?

Having made it this far, you may be wondering, What *really* happens next? Plans are great, but how does planning play out when we actually start the hard work of implementing a plan? What if things change that we didn't expect? While we can't address every possible scenario, we can draw on our fifty-four museum master plans to suggest some common outcomes.

In our experience, what happens next falls into multiple categories:

- *Immediate success:* Everything falls into place, and two or three years after the master plan is completed, a new or revitalized museum opens. Unfortunately, this only happens in a small percentage of projects.
- *Fundraising challenges:* A project stalls because of fundraising issues, but then it restarts with new leadership who can better articulate the need for the project.
- *Death and rebirth:* A major change within the organization puts the plan on the shelf, only for it to resurface twenty years later in doing research for a subsequent master planning process. Some version of death and rebirth happens to as many as a third of our projects.
- *Surprise!* An unexpected turn of events (a new collection, a generous new donor, an offer of real estate) sends the museum off in a different direction. This happens more frequently than you might expect, but it is usually a welcome, if unusual, outcome.
- *Incremental Progress:* The project begins fundraising, searching for a site, or other next steps identified in the plan. Progress is steady, but not dramatic. Sometimes there are unanticipated roadblocks and lengthy detours. And other times, there is immediate support and generous funding. In our experience, incremental progress is the most common outcome.

Very rarely is a master plan completely abandoned. Some portion of it, or some idea that was embedded in it, usually comes to life and transforms a part of the museum's work. The goals of a master plan are often lofty, and they may take fifteen to twenty years to fully accomplish, even when the museum is well resourced. Museum Insights completed the first master plan for the Academy Museum of Motion Pictures in 2008; the museum did not open to the public until 2021. Patience, steady effort, and a never-say-die attitude pay dividends in the end. Of course, some museums do fail. We close this book with a consideration of two museum failures, both of which help to demonstrate the benefits of a constituent-focused planning approach.

Perhaps the most common cause of museum failure is the "If we build it, they will come" fallacy. In museums, this often plays out as "If we build it, they will come, and the admission fees and gift shop revenue will fund the museum." "If we build it, they will come" may work in the movies, but it doesn't often work in the museum business, where the average cost per visitor for a museum is double the revenue from the ticket sales. The Sports Museum of America, formerly in New York City, is a good example of this fallacy.

The Sports Museum of America had an ambitious plan to create a for-profit museum that celebrated America's love of sports. Located in New York City and funded in part by investors, the museum would be located on Wall Street in lower Manhattan on the second floor of an existing office building. The museum was designed with a variety of static and immersive exhibits about a wide variety of sports. The founders were particularly excited about being a new home for the Heisman Trophy. Attendance was projected to be a million visitors a year, largely drawn from the city's thriving tourist market. Interest-free bonds, granted to support the redevelopment of the area following the 9/11 attacks, would cover the initial cost of the museum, and then, they projected, it would earn enough from admissions to repay the loans.[1]

Clearly, the goal was to be a Destination Museum catering to tourists, but the location belied that choice. Few of the millions of NYC tourists visit Wall Street. Those who do are likely to be interested in the New York Stock Exchange, not a sports museum. Even if they were interested, they might easily miss the museum since it had little visible presence at street level. The museum opened in May 2008 and closed less than nine months later, in February 2009, having attracted fewer than 125,000 actual visitors.[2] The causes of its failure are relatively clear: overly optimistic attendance projections compounded by a very poor choice of location meant that the destination business model was unlikely to work. For a museum with ambitious attendance-driven goals, a location on or near the city's tourist-rich Museum Mile might have been more appropriate. Most museum failures, though, are both more complex and play out over years, not months.

The American Textile History Museum's demise took a different course. To paraphrase Hemingway, it failed slowly at first, and then all at once. The museum was founded as the Merrimack Valley Textile Museum in North Andover, Massachusetts, in 1960 by Caroline Stevens Rogers, a member of a significant textile industry family and recognized as a skilled hand weaver and textile dyer in her own right.[3] The museum achieved AAM accreditation in 1973. For the next thirty years, the museum focused on collecting textiles, supporting research, and producing curatorial publications. The Textile Conservation Center, founded in 1977, was the cornerstone of the museum's work to become a leading center for the study of textiles in the United States. This work also established a very clear Curatorial operating model. Running short of space for its ever-expanding collections, in 1997 the museum opened in a new space in Lowell, near the Lowell National Historical Park, home to some of America's first water-powered textile mills.[4]

This relocation also marked a change in focus. Building on work begun in the 1980s, the museum sought to appeal to a wider public through a significant expansion of education programs for both regional students and adults, as well as with general public-facing exhibits in its new location. This new business model had mixed success, and the museum was not able to support the cost of operations. In 2007, the museum underwent a restructuring, including closing its textile conservation lab (and ceding its original curatorial role), and investing heavily in new exhibits.[5] With new exhibits, the museum strove to build attendance and generate operating support, but it was unable to sustain the new model. The museum closed in June 2016 due to ongoing operating deficits.[6]

The fate of the American Textile History Museum (ATHM) reveals two common mistakes. First, the museum lost sight of its most important constituents—the Curatorial constituents who had founded the museum and supported it for its first thirty years. While museums should grow and change over time, change needs to be made with a clear understanding of those whom the museum will serve and the requirements of the resulting operating model. Changes within the museum's core focus on a specific part of the guitar-pick diagram are often productive; wild swings from corner to corner of the guitar pick are likely warning signs of a museum that has lost its focus. This appears to be the case here, as the museum made a radical shift from Curatorial to Community, signaled by the closing of the textile conservation lab. Shortly after, the museum swung again, this time from Community to Destination, leading Community and Curatorial constituents to question the museum's commitment to them and perplexing prospective Destination constituents, who didn't understand why the museum had value—or how it was distinct from the National Park Service exhibits they would encounter down the street.

The second common mistake was failing to understand the business models aligned with each type of museum. The ATHM's founder left an endowment that supported operating like a Curatorial museum, but not enough to also support the public programming and outreach (and associated staffing and overhead) typical of a Community Museum. While the museum's 2008 capital campaign added one million dollars to the endowment, the Community Museum model still could not sustain operating expenses. The instinct of the museum's remaining stakeholders was to earn their way back to operating stability, a difficult task for most museums, but perhaps impossible for a museum with a large collection to care for. The earnings from a Destination Museum model simply weren't enough to keep the doors open, the lights on, and the collections-storage HVAC system running.

A note, though, that hindsight is twenty-twenty. The museum made these changes at a time when the call from the museum world was for museums to be leaders in education and public programming, rather than simply repositories for objects. While sticking to their knitting was probably the more prudent course, doing so in practice is harder than it sounds, as this case study shows. The bottom line is that museums reach their full potential when their business model aligns with and addresses the interests, needs, and desires of their primary constituents. Understanding who these constituents are and what they want is at the heart of successful master planning.

If planning is no guarantee of immediate success (or even success at all!), then why plan? Because, as Dwight Eisenhower memorably said, "Plans are worthless, but planning is everything."[7] We believe that planning produces two critical outcomes that will serve your organization well, regardless of what happens next. The first outcome, as Eisenhower noted, is the act of planning itself and the learning you take away from the process. The act of planning forces you to set a clear direction that carefully considers the museum's most important outcomes, potential obstacles (and how to overcome them), what can be left by the wayside, and what might be foreseeable complications to implementing the plan. As important, planning forces you to make a case for your organization's future. It provides staff, board, and key stakeholders with a clear sense of direction. They understand those whom your organization serves and the desired outcomes. This shared sense of purpose will help the organization weather the challenges that will inevitably arise as you work to implement the master plan.

The second outcome is understanding your most important constituents. Understanding constituents, and articulating their interests, needs, motivations, and desires, may be the most enduring aspect of the planning process. When a museum's stakeholders understand those whom the museum serves and the outcomes from serving them well, it will be well-positioned for success. Regardless of what curveballs the real world hurls at your plan, you can always return to your core constituents. If the museum takes thoughtful actions that serve its key constituents, the museum will be more likely to succeed, even if the specific actions have little resemblance to the original plan.

When in doubt, ask the questions, "Who are we doing this for?" and, "What are the outcomes that will indicate success for our museum as we've defined them?" Decisions made with these questions in mind will keep the museum on track for the goals established in the master plan, even if the newly charted course looks to be very different. Having thought these matters over carefully through the planning process, you are prepared to launch your best effort, whether it is D-Day or an expansion to the education wing. Whatever you are undertaking, your effort will benefit from your planning work. We're rooting for you.

Onward!

NOTES

1. Bill Pennington, "Sports Museum and Heisman Find Place in Lower Manhattan," *New York Times*, April 13, 2005, https://www.nytimes.com/2005/04/13/sports/ncaafootball/sports-museum-and-heisman-find-place-in-lower-manhattan.html (accessed August 18, 2024).
2. Richard Sandomir, "Financial Problems Close Sports Museum," *New York Times*, February 20, 2009, https://www.nytimes.com/2009/02/21/sports/21museum.html (accessed August 18, 2024).
3. American Textile History Museum, "Mission and History," American Textile History Museum, https://web.archive.org/web/20170722222242/http://www.athm.org/about-athm/mission-history/ (accessed via internet archive, August 20, 2024).
4. Ibid.
5. Ibid.
6. American Textile History Museum [successor organization not affiliated with the original], "ATHM to Close Permanently," American Textile History Museum, https://www.athm.org/news/athm-seeks-to-close/ (accessed August 15, 2024).
7. The American Presidency Project, "Dwight D. Eisenhower: Remarks at the National Defense Executive Reserve Conference," UC Santa Barbara, https://www.presidency.ucsb.edu/documents/remarks-the-national-defense-executive-reserve-conference (accessed August 9, 2024).

Index

AAM. *See* American Alliance of Museums
AASLH. *See* American Association for State and Local History
academic and research centers, 33
The Academy Museum of Motion Pictures, 13-14, *14*, 111
accessibility, 65, 95
active season programs, 68
activist museums, 33
Activity and Experience Plan: categories for, 57-58; collections and curation, 64-65; community-building events, 62-63; for Community Museum, 68-71; crafting, 65-72; creating, 58-65; engagement with partner or parent organizations, 60-61; for Historic House Museum, *66-68*; internships, fellowships, and apprenticeships, 63; online happenings/virtual engagement, 64; Preliminary Space Needs Outline and, 84; public programs, 61; research and publications, 64; revenue projection and, 75; seasonal, 68-71; staffing projection based on, 77; template, *66-71*; tour or docent-led experiences, 60
adaptability, sustainability and, xvi
administration, space for operations and, 92
affinity community museums, 11, 13
Alice Paul Institute, 33
amenities, 74
American Alliance of Museums (AAM), 105
American Association for State and Local History (AASLH), 105
American Textile History Museum (ATHM), 112-13
apprenticeships, 63
architects, 83, 100, 106-8
Art Complex Museum, *16*, 16-17
assessment: Drucker on organizational, 4; established museum facility, 88-92;

logic model and facility, 89-91; museum classroom, 90; new museum facility needs, 83-88; site, 86-88, *88*; site evaluation worksheet, 94-97; staffing, 77; template for facility, *89*
Association of Science and Technology Centers (ASTC), 105
ATHM. *See* American Textile History Museum
attraction, clubhouse *vs.*, xiv

background research, 19-20
back-of-house support, 65
benchmarking, 22; case studies, 32-33; gathering comparable financial data, 29-30; interview questions, *34-35*; making initial list, 28-29; misunderstandings and mismatches, 33; one-third model and, 35n1; overview, 25; picking institutions for, 25-28; putting it all together, *31-32*, 31-35, *31*, *32*; questions, 28, 29; similar institutions, 26; ways to use, 32
board members, 19, 42
book club, 69
brainstorming, constituent group identifying, 37-38, *41*
branch institutes, 5-6
bucket list visitors, 38
budget: contingency funds, 86; new museum preliminary, 83-88, *87*; staff percentage of, 74
buildings: benchmark questions on facilities and, *34-35*; Class A, 85; code consultants and, 106; short-term cost implications for existing, 95
burnout, 79
bus access, 88
business planning, xv

café, museum, 74
capital, budget for preliminary, 85-86, *87*

Carnegie Museum of Natural History, 11
case studies: The Academy Museum of Motion Pictures, 13-14, *14*; The Art Complex Museum, *16*, 16-17; benchmarking and, 32-34; Center for Puppetry Arts, 15-16
CD. *See* Construction Documents
Center for Community Health and Development, 45
Center for Puppetry Arts, 15-16
Center for Ray Bradbury Studies, 33
center of gravity, 12, 34, 41
challenges: constituent classification, 39; definition of, 21; fundraising, 111. *See also* Resources, Constraints, Challenges, and Opportunities framework
children, 2, 5. *See also* K-12 students
citizen science programs, 63
Class A buildings, 85
classroom, sample assessment of museum, 90
client, being strong, 100
clubhouse, attraction *vs.*, xiv
Clyfford Still Museum, 11
collections: benchmark questions on, *34-35*; circulation, 103; curation and, 64-65; Dana on museum, 5, 6; focus on people instead of, 1; planning for, 103; space list for, 92-93; storage costs, 80
Community Museum (community-engaged museums), 60; Activity and Experience Plan excerpt for, 68-71; benchmarking and, 33; changing from Curatorial to, 113; characteristics, 10-11; community-building events, 62-63, 70; community outreach, 70; constituent group, 38-39; in Constituent Logic Model template, *46*; constituent motivations and needs, 41; constituents, xv, 10-11, 41, 42, 66; Historic House Museums and, 66; operating implications for, *13*; revenue sources, 75; subtypes, 11; tourist-focused *vs.*, xiv
Community Tool Box, 45
concept design, 106, 108
Concept of the Corporation (Drucker), 3
constituent groups, identifying: checklist for interviewee selection, 40; classification challenges, 39; Community, 38-39; Curatorial, 39; Destination, 38; interviewing, 40-44; motivations and needs of, 41; overlapping, 39
Constituent Logic Model: column 1: constituents, 47; column 2: needs, motivations, and desires, 47, *46*; column 3: activities and experiences, 48; column 4: operational needs, 48-49; column 5: facility needs, 49; column 6: outcomes, 50; developing, 46-52, *46*, *51-52*; guitar pick diagram and, 53; logic model definition and, 45-46; narrowing down constituents in, 53; purpose of, 45; sample completed, *51-52*; template, *46*; using, 53
constituents: benchmarking museums with similar, 26; categories of, xv; changing original focus and, 112-13; defining, 37-39; interviews with, 39-41; overlapping, 39; primary customers, 3, 4; understanding, xv; use of term, xvi; visitors *vs.*, 37. *See also* Activity and Experience Plan; *specific museum types*
constraints, 20-21
construction: estimates *vs.* actual costs, 97; estimating preliminary costs, 85
Construction Documents (CD), 106, 108
consultants: acoustic, 107; code, 106; economic feasibility, 73, 74; fundraising, 99, 101-2; selection process, 105; space planners, 83, 100, 102-3; types, 99-100
contingency funds, 86
contract curators, 100
copy room, 93
courses, 69
COVID-19, 22, 30
curation: collections and, 64-65; community, 70; contract curators, 100
Curatorial Museum, 60; changing to Community from, 113; in Constituent Logic Model template, *46*; constituent motivations and needs, 41; constituents, xv, 39; defining characteristics, 11; operating implications for, *13*; revenue sources, 75

Dana, John Cotton, 1-6
DD. *See* Design Development
DEAI. *See* Diversity, Equity, Accessibility, and Inclusion
debt, fundraising and, 108-9
Denver Art Museum, 104
Denver Public Library, 2
Design Development (DD), 106, 108
designers: architects and, 100; interior, 107; interpretive planners and exhibit, 104-6; lighting, 107; selecting design professional or architect, 107-8

design stages, 108
Destination Museum: in Constituent Logic Model template, 46; constituents of, xv, 10, 38, 41; example of failed, 112; exhibit costs for new, 86; motivation and needs of constituents, 41; operating implications for, 13; revenue sources, 75
"dirty" exhibit staging area, 93
"discovery," 19-20
Diversity, Equity, Accessibility, and Inclusion (DEAI), 22, 38, 65; Facility Plan and, 89; staffing projection and, 80
documentation: Construction Documents, 106, 108; planning team document package, 20
donations, 76
donors, constituent interviews with, 42
Drucker, Peter, 1, 3-4, 7n12

economic feasibility consultant, 73, 74
education: areas, 93; department staff, 62
Eisenhower, Dwight, 113
Emily Dickinson Museum, 11
engineers, 106, 109
Eric Carle Museum of Picture Book Art, 1
evening meetups, 70
executive leadership, 19
exhibit designers, 104-6
exhibits: benchmark questions on, 34; costs for long-term, 86; facility assessment for areas of, 92-93; long-term, 86, 97n3; need for updating, 97n3; "permanent," 97n3; programs for temporary, 68-69; temporary or traveling, 59-60, 66
expansion, 80-81

facilities: benchmark questions on building and, 35; citizen science programs and, 63; Constituent Logic Model column on, 46, 49, 50; creative ways to address needs of, 91; DEAI work and, 92; facility assessment for established museums, 88-92; Facility Plan, 89; government, 76; Historic House Museum requirements, 66, 68; needs assessment for new museums, 83-88; planning, 83; planning for future growth, 88; for season programs, 71; site evaluation worksheet, 94-97; space planners and, 83, 102-3; for visitor reception, 59
failures, museum, 27-28, 97n2, 111-12
families: programs for youth and, 62; weekend programming for, 70

feasibility study, fundraising consultants and, 101-2
fellowships, 63
film museum, xiii-xiv. *See also* Academy Museum of Motion Pictures
finances: benchmarking and, 29-30; Constituent Logic Model and, 46; cost per visitor, 74; expense projection, 77-81; lending and, 6; marketing costs, 74; mission and money outcomes, 41, 46, 50, *51-52*; most significant expense, 30; outcomes by constituent group, 47; record storage, 93; revenue projection, 74-77; soft costs, 85-86; template for tracking, 32; VE for cutting costs, 109. *See also* staffing and operational needs
The Five Most Important Questions You Will Ever Ask About Your Organization (Drucker), 3
Floyd, George, 22
focus groups, 40
Folger Shakespeare Library, 33
Form 990, IRS, 29
fundraising: challenges, 111; consultants, 99, 101-2; debt and, 108-9; grants and, 76

gift shop, 74
The Gloom of the Museum (Dana), 2
government facilities, 76
grandparent days, 69
grants, 76
Gross Square Feet (GSF), 84
group interviews, 40
GSF. *See* Gross Square Feet
GuideStar, 29
guitar pick diagram, *12, 14, 15, 16,* 34; danger of swinging across, 112

Halls of Fame, 10
Harriet Beecher Stowe Center, 33
Historic House Museum, 28, 33; Activity and Experience Plan for, *66-68*; sample logic model for, *46*
history, community, 70
history museums, categories for, 58
hobby historians, 70

independent literary centers, 33
initial staffing model, 79-80
interior designers, 107
internships, 63, 78
interpretive planners, 100, 104-6

Index 117

interviews: candidate selection checklist, 42; constituent, 39–41, 42; questions for benchmark, *34–35*; sample interview discussion guide, 43–44; selection checklist for constituent, 40; tips for scheduling and conducting, 42–43
IRS Form 990, 18n7, 29, 30

jamboards, 38

K-12 students: activities and experiences sample list, 48; bus access, 88; Constituent Logic Model columns on, 47, 48, 49, 50; facility needs and, 49–50; needs and motivations of, 49; operational needs related to, 49; programs for school groups, 61–62

landscape architects, 106
landscape tour, Historic House Museum, 67
leadership: executive, 19; interview with local, 42; team, 19
lending, 6
Let's Talk about It, 70
libraries: independent literary centers and, 33; reform, 2
lighting designers, 107
Lincoln's Cottage, 33
literary figures, logic model for historic house museum and, *51–52*
literary museums: connected to university, 33; independent centers, 33
loading dock, 93, 100
location, 73; accessible, 95
logic model, 45–46; completed sample by constituent group, *51–52*; facilities column of, 83; facility assessment in light of, 89–91; Preliminary Space Needs Outline and, 84; revenue projection adjustments based on, 75; sample summarized, *54–55*; template, *46*. See also Constituent Logic Model
lunches, brown-bag weekly, 69

MAAM. *See* Mid-Atlantic Association of Museums
maintenance and repair, 74, 93, 95
Managing the Non-Profit Organization (Drucker), 3
Marine Corps Museum, 10
marketing costs, 74
Mark Twain Boyhood Home, 33
master planning, museum: background research, 19–20; compiling master plan, 92–97; critical aspects of, xv–xvi; development phases, xvi; next steps after, 111–13; people-centered, 1, 9–10; practical foundations of, 19–23; successful, xv–xvi, 1–3, 111; surprise element, 111; team development, 19; user-focused approach to, xiv–xvi. *See also specific topics*
Merrimack Valley Textile Museum, 112
Mid-Atlantic Association of Museums (MAAM), 105
Midwest prairie, xiv–xv
mission and money outcomes, 41, 50, *52*, 53, *55*
museums: case studies on types of, 13–17, *14*; center of gravity, 12, 34, 41; challenges faced by today's, 4–5; commonality shared by, 9; community vs. tourist-focused, *xiv*; constituents focus, xv–xvi; Dana principles of effective, 5–6; death and rebirth, 111; differences between, xiii, xv; Drucker organization ideas applied to, 3–4; failed, 27–28, 97n2, 111–12; new, 73, 81, 83–88; organization with four, xiii; overlapping types of, 11–12, *12*, *14*, *15*; problem with serving "everyone," 9–10; with similar subject matter, 26; survey of U.S., 2; types of, 10–13, *12*, *13*, 17n1; with unusual shared characteristics, 27. *See also* master planning, museum; *specific types of museums*

National Drag Racing Hall of Fame, 75
National Park Service, xv
National Steinbeck Center, 33
Nature Conservancy, xv
NEMA. *See* New England Museum Association
Net Square Feet (NSF), 84, *87*
Net Usable Area (Net Area), 84
New England Museum Association (NEMA), 105
The New Museum (Dana), 3, 5–6
new museums, 73, 81; establishing facility needs and preliminary budget, 83–88; planning for future growth, 88; site selection criteria, 86–88
nonprofits (not-for-profits), 3–4; revenue streams, 75
NSF. *See* Net Square Feet

one-third model, 35n1
online activities, 64
operations: Constituent Logic Model and, *46*; Constituent Logic Model column on, 48–49;

Historic House Museum, 66, 68; implications by museum type, *13*; projecting costs, 80–81; season programs and, 71; space for administration and, 93. *See also* staffing and operational needs

OPM. *See* Owners' Project Manager

organizations: assessment of, 4; constituent interviews with partner, 42; Drucker concept of people and, 3–4; engagement with partner or parent, 60–61; hosted programs for partner, 69

orientation, visitor, 58–59

The Oscars Experience, 14

outdoor: characteristics, 94; recreation, 95; space needs, 84

Owners' Project Manager (OPM), 86, 100, 109–10

parking, 94

partner organizations, constituent interviews with, 42

passion tax, 79

people, focus on, 1. *See also* constituents

phases, master planning, xvi

planning. *See* business planning; museum master planning

progress, incremental, 111

ProPublica, 29

publications, research and, 64

public programs, 61, 68, 93

puppetry, 15–16

questions: to asking organizations, 3; benchmark, 28, 29, *34–35*

recreation, outdoor, 95

regional community museums, 11, 13, 71

Request for Proposals (RFP), 105, 108

Request for Qualifications (RFQ), 105, 108

research: Activity and Experience Plan and, 64; background, 19–20; publications and, 64. *See also* scholars and researchers

Resources, Constraints, Challenges, and Opportunities framework, 20–22, *23*

revenue: ability to generate, 96; creating initial revenue projection, 75–77; not-for-profit, 75; projecting, 74–77; sources, 75; typical sources of, 76

RFP. *See* Request for Proposals

RFQ. *See* Request for Qualifications

risk, 91

Rock & Roll Hall of Fame, 12

Rogers, Caroline Stevens, 112

Rosenbach Library, 33

Schematic Design (SD), 106, 108

scholars and researchers, 39, 47, 48, 49, 50

schools: Dana on, 5; out-of-school programs, 62; program for school groups, 61–62. *See also* classroom, sample assessment of museum

science, citizen science programs, 63

SD. *See* Schematic Design

seasonality, 68–71, 78

self-guided tour, Historic House Museum, 67

site evaluation: sample score sheet, *96–97*; worksheet, *94–97*

site-selection: assessment, 86–88, *88*; scoring table, *88*; site evaluation worksheet, 94–97

size, 26

Smithsonian Museums, museum types and, 10

soft costs, 85–86

space: allocation, xiv, *xiv*; preliminary museum space list, *92–93*; spaces that don't work, 90

Space-Needs Outline, preliminary, 84, 85, 86

space planners, 83, 100, 102–3

Sports Museum of America, 112

staff, 96; adding operational, 78; benchmark questions on, *35*; burnout, 79; constituent interviews with, 42; Constituent Logic Model and, *46*; cost percentage of operating budget, 74; education department, 62; full-time, part-time, and seasonal, 78; identifying staffing needs, 77; initial staffing model, 79–80; other staffing considerations, 110; partner organizations requirement for, 60; pay, 79; percentage of overall expenses, 77; review of existing, 79–80; staffing assessment table, 77; staffing for K-12 students, 49; succession planning, 79; template for benchmarking facility and, *35*; temporary, 110

staffing and operational needs: DEAI and, 80; existing *vs.* new museums and, 73; initial projections, 73; projecting expenses, 77–81; projecting revenue, 74–77; rules of thumb, 74

storage: collections, 80; financial and other records, 93; temporary, 93

story-centric museums, 104

story time, 69

Strengths, Weaknesses, Opportunities, and Threats (SWOT) framework, 21–22

Index 119

sustainability, adaptability and, xvi
SWOT. *See* Strengths, Weaknesses, Opportunities, and Threats

teachers, 61
team, master planning, 110; constituent identification brainstorming session with, 37–38; developing, 19; leadership, 19
templates: Activity and Experience Plan, 72; benchmarking, *31*, 31–35, *31, 32*; brainstorming session homework, *41*; facility assessment, *89*; financial tracking table, *32*; museum attendance and entry fee tracking, *31*; preliminary museum space list, *92–93*; staff and facility tracking, *32*; staffing assessment, 77
Textile Conservation Center, 112
tourist-focused museums, community-focused *vs.*, *xiv*
tours, 60, 67

universities, literary museum connected to, 32–33
University of Kansas, 45
user-focused approach, xiv–xvi

Value Engineering (VE), 109
virtual engagement, 64
visitors: benchmark questions on tracking, *34*; bucket list, 38; constituents *vs.*, 37; cost per visitor, 74; museum attendance and entry fee tracking, *31*; reception and orientation, 58–59; repeat, 11; services areas, 92; visiting friends and relatives, 47, 48, 49, 50. *See also* constituents, served by museums
volunteers, 7n12, 63–64, 78

weekly lunches, 69
workshop, maintenance, 93
World of Coke, 10
Wren's Nest, 33

youth, 62

About the Authors

Guy Hermann is the principal at Museum Insights, a museum master planning firm based in Massachusetts. Guy brings twenty-five years of master planning experience built on fifteen years working in museum education and operations to his planning projects. His more than fifty master plans range from a visitor-experience master plan for Harlem's Apollo Theater, to developing a master site plan for the Emily Dickinson Museum, to working with the Academy leadership to plan the Academy Museum of Motion Pictures in Los Angeles.

Sara Patton Zarrelli is a public historian committed to helping museums and historic sites develop a sense of place through exhibits, landscapes, and experiences that meaningfully connect visitors to the messy realities of the past and the present. She has worked for the National Park Service, the Trustees of Reservations, and Historic New England. Since 2019, she has been a museum planner with Museum Insights. Project highlights include creating an award-winning assessment matrix for Connecticut Landmarks, providing project management for exhibits at the Art Complex Museum, and creating operating policies for the National Coast Guard Museum.

www.ingramcontent.com/pod-product-compliance
Lightning Source LLC
Chambersburg PA
CBHW060515300426
44112CB00017B/2676